Ralph David Abernathy

Ralph David Abernathy

by
Catherine Reef

A People in Focus Book

 **DILLON PRESS**
Parsippany, New Jersey

Acknowledgments

Quotations on pages 13, 15, 31, 84, 100, 123, 128, and 132 are from VOICES OF FREEDOM by Henry Hampton and Steve Fayer. Copyright © 1990 by Blackside, Inc. Used by permission of Bantam Books, a division of Bantam Doubleday Dell Publishing Group, Inc.

Quotations on pages 24, 27, 28, 30, 31-32, 40, 45, 48, 52, 66-67, 81, 86, 88, 103, 104, and 121-122 are from AND THE WALLS CAME TUMBLING DOWN by Ralph D. Abernathy. Copyright © 1989 by Ralph David Abernathy.

Photo Credits

Cover: Dennis Brack/Black Star
Back Cover: Richard Lawrence Stack/Black Star

AP/Wide World: 14. Bettmann: 13, 17, 59, 62, 108, 111, 136, 155, 159. Black Star: Dennis Brack, 71; Matt Herron, 53; Charles Moore, 87. Culver Pictures: 15, 97. Magnum: Henri Cartier Bresson, 120; Bruce Davidson, 124; Danny Lyon, 83, 91. Strictly Black & White: 80, 114. Take Stock: Matt Herron, 44.

Library of Congress Cataloging-in-Publication Data

Reef, Catherine.
    Ralph David Abernathy/by Catherine Reef.—1st ed.
      p. cm.—(People in focus book)
    Includes bibliographical references (p.) and index.
    ISBN 0-87518-653-X   ISBN 0-382-24965-8 pbk
    1. Abernathy, Ralph, 1926–1990—Juvenile literature. 2. King, Martin Luther, Jr., 1929–1968—Juvenile literature. 3. Afro-Americans—Biography—Juvenile literature. 4. Civil rights workers—United States—Biography—Juvenile literature. 5. Afro-Americans—Civil rights—Juvenile literature. 6. Civil rights movements—United States—History—20th century—Juvenile literature. [1. Abernathy, Ralph, 1926–1990. 2. Civil rights workers. 3. Afro-Americans—Biography. 4. Civil rights movements—History.] I. Title. II. Series.
E185.97.A13R44 1995
323'.092—dc20
[B]   94-28623

Summary: A biography of Martin Luther King's second in command in the civil rights movement, including Abernathy's role after King's untimely death.

Published by Dillon Press, an imprint of Silver Burdett Press.
A Simon & Schuster Company
299 Jefferson Road, Parsippany, NJ 07054

First edition

Printed in Mexico

10 9 8 7 6 5 4 3 2 1

/ Contents

Introduction		7
Chapter One	Into the Promised Land	11
Chapter Two	The Barefoot Boy	23
Chapter Three	Taking His Place	35
Chapter Four	God's Plan	49
Chapter Five	Walk Together Children	63
Chapter Six	Keep Moving, Birmingham	77
Chapter Seven	Jericho	95
Chapter Eight	This Lonesome Valley	115
Chapter Nine	Raising Questions	133
Chapter Ten	The Giant-slayer	150
Selected Bibliography		162
Index		165

/ Introduction

One of the greatest pleasures of my life is being the second-born son of Ralph David Abernathy. Not only was he my father, but he was my best friend as well. Just as he was a friend to me, he was a friend to humankind. My father was one of the founders of the American civil rights movement. He was a great theologian and a philosopher of love and nonviolence. He started the civil rights movement after Rosa Parks was arrested. He organized the first meeting that led to the Montgomery, Alabama, bus boycott.

As chairman of the Montgomery Improvement Association, my father drafted the first resolution of the civil rights movement, just hours after Rosa Park's arrest. He asked for courteous treatment by bus drivers; a first-come, first-served seating policy; and African American bus operators on predominantly "Negro" routes. These requests for human dignity were so simple, yet the spiritual demands they imposed were so great.

Martin Luther King, Jr., recalled that historic first meeting in his book *Stride Toward Freedom*. He wrote that, after Ralph David Abernathy read the resolution calling for African Americans to boycott the buses of Montgomery, " . . . every person to a man stood up. . . . Cheers began to ring out from both inside and outside. I had never seen such enthusiasm for freedom." King continued, "The victory is already won, no matter how long we struggle to attain the three points of this resolution. It is a victory infinitely larger than the bus situation. The real victory was in the mass meeting, where thousands of Black people stood revealed with a new sense of dignity and destiny."

The civil rights movement of the 1950s and 1960s ended with Ralph Abernathy, also. The very last protest and demonstration was the Poor People's Campaign, in 1968. He led thousands of people to Washington, D.C., where they camped out near the Lincoln Memorial. In this way, he brought the plight of the poor before the nation and Congress.

As a child, I watched my father motivate thousands of people to stand up courageously and fight against segregation and oppression. Unrelentingly, he fought for integration with his "closest and dearest" friend, Martin Luther King. They worked as a team and were known in their day as "the civil rights twins."

At my father's funeral, the Reverend Jesse Jackson said, "If Martin was our leader, then Ralph was our pastor." Ralph David Abernathy was Martin's pastor, too. He was also his leader and confidant. He embodied the principles of nonviolence and God's creative, redemptive love, which he taught by example to everyone. He was a man who lived what he preached. He said that none of us is greater than another in the eyes of God, and that we are all brethren.

Ralph David Abernathy was a man of God first and foremost, and then a servant of the people. He said that as a little boy he met God in a meadow one day. He decided then to become a preacher of God's word. Little did he know that he would change the lives of millions of Americans.

From the start of the bus boycott in 1955 until his death on April 17, 1990, Ralph David Abernathy dedicated his life to serving his fellow human beings. He asked for nothing but freedom for his people in return. Truly, he is the unsung hero of the civil rights movement. He hoped that one day we would all live together in peace and love, as brothers and sisters. My father said, "We hate each other because we fear each other. We fear each other because we won't sit down at the table together." His personal motto was "Freedom is not simply the right to do as you please, but freedom is when it pleases you to do what is right!"

My father lived his life wanting to create a better tomorrow for everyone. His epitaph reads,

Chapter / One

Into the Promised Land

It was a Monday in April 1968. Main Street in Memphis, Tennessee, was crowded with people. It was a scene like many that had been acted out in Southern cities during the 1950s and 1960s. Men, women, and children, both black and white, were marching for equality for African Americans.

But anyone who had viewed the civil rights marches of the past could see that this one was different. In the past, the demonstrators had sung hymns and songs of freedom as they marched. "I woke up this morning with my mind stayed on freedom"—lyrics such as these expressed commitment and hope. This time, however, the marchers moved silently.

Just a few days earlier, the Reverend Martin Luther King, Jr., had been shot and killed in this Mississippi River port. King had led black Americans in many peaceful protests over the past 13 years. He had led them in a great struggle to break down barriers of hatred and discrimination. Now, suddenly, he was gone. The silence of this march was in memory of him.

The Reverend Ralph David Abernathy led the line of moving people. Abernathy looked at the hushed witnesses who lined the sidewalk on either side. To the right and to the left, he saw stunned, sorrowful faces, faces that mourned the fallen civil rights leader. Abernathy had an added reason to mourn. With the death of Martin Luther King, Jr., he had lost his best friend.

Ralph Abernathy and Martin Luther King, Jr., had been together since the earliest days of the civil rights movement, when they were both young Baptist ministers in Montgomery, Alabama. They had grown up in the segregated South, in a social system that kept blacks apart from whites. This segregation locked many blacks in poverty and robbed them of their fundamental rights.

In the late 1970s, Abernathy was interviewed for a television series on the civil rights movement called "Eyes on the Prize." He spoke about what it

Mourners line a road in Atlanta, Georgia, as the mule-drawn caisson bearing the body of Dr. Martin Luther King, Jr., passes en route to Morehouse College, site of a memorial service.

was like to live under segregation. "Blacks were permitted to hold only the menial jobs, domestic workers and common and ordinary laborers," Abernathy said. "We were the last to be hired and the first to be fired."

The system denied African Americans the basic dignity to which all citizens are entitled. "All of the restaurants were segregated, the hotels and motels were segregated. Meaning that black people were not permitted to live in these hotels," Abernathy explained in the interview. "Even in the public courthouse, blacks could not drink

Ralph Abernathy and Martin Luther King, Jr., in the early days of the civil rights movement

A banner carried in the March on Washington in August 1963

water except from the fountain labeled 'colored.' "

The segregation extended to city bus systems, where seating for African Americans was restricted. In 1955, Abernathy and King led a bus boycott in the city of Montgomery. Under their guidance, Montgomery's African Americans refused to ride the municipal buses until they were guaranteed fair treatment. The protest resulted in a civil rights milestone—the outlawing of segregation on public transportation throughout the United States. It also launched a historic movement in which millions of people worked for racial equality in American society.

As the civil rights movement gained momentum, Abernathy and King proved to be an effective team. They formed an organization, the

Southern Christian Leadership Conference, dedicated to nonviolent change. With King as president and Abernathy as secretary-treasurer, the
Southern Christian Leadership Conference did
much to improve life for black Americans.

In Birmingham, Alabama, their demonstrations brought integration to downtown businesses.
In Selma, Alabama, they marched to guarantee
blacks the right to vote. In those cities and elsewhere, the Southern Christian Leadership
Conference made gains that benefited blacks in
every American community. The organization's
work led to federal laws protecting civil rights.

Abernathy and King often traveled together
over the years. They marched together and prayed
together. They even went to jail together. These
experiences helped their friendship grow deeper
and stronger. King wrote about Abernathy in his
book on the Montgomery bus boycott, *Stride
Toward Freedom*. From the first days of the civil
rights movement, King wrote, "Ralph Abernathy
was my closest associate and most trusted friend."

King was frequently in the public eye. His
speeches, eloquent and dotted with quotes from
philosophers, received national attention.
Abernathy worked largely behind the scenes,
organizing meetings, planning demonstrations,

Martin Luther King, Jr., and Ralph Abernathy after being arrested for their integration attempts at restaurants in St. Augustine, Florida and developing the strategies that would result in landmark changes. Before making decisions, King often turned to Abernathy for advice.

Raised on an Alabama farm, Ralph Abernathy addressed crowds in plain, everyday terms. His down-to-earth sense of humor enlivened many of his speeches. Andrew Young, the civil rights worker who was elected mayor of Atlanta, Georgia, in 1981, commented on Abernathy's ability to connect with the common people. "The brothers in the street," Young told the *New York Times*, "remember the things he says, even when they don't know his name or who he is." Young summed up Abernathy's speaking talent this way: "Ralph can talk the language."

"Ralph's slow movements and slow, easy talk were deceptive," King explained in *Stride Toward Freedom*. "For he was an indefatigable worker and a sound thinker, possessed of a fertile mind." Abernathy spoke slowly and carefully so that every listener could hear his words and understand their meaning.

King had named Abernathy to take his place as president of the Southern Christian Leadership Conference in the event of his death. Abernathy had expected he would never have to do this. A successful assassination attempt would take both men's lives, he had believed, because he and King were so often together. And, in fact, Abernathy had been just footsteps away when a bullet claimed Martin Luther King's life.

"I never thought the day would come I'd have to live without Martin," he said in a 1968 interview. New to leadership, Abernathy felt the burden of going it alone, a burden King never had to carry.

A solid man, 5 feet 8 inches tall, Abernathy brought the silent marchers to Memphis City Hall and mounted the steps to address them. He turned to his audience, resolved to do his best as their leader.

Abernathy was a deeply religious man who often drew parallels between the events of his day and stories from the Bible. He compared the African American quest for equal treatment to the ancient Hebrews' search for their promised land. According to the Bible, Moses led the Hebrews out of Egypt, where they had lived in exile. The Hebrews wandered in the desert for 40 years before finding their true home, their promised land.

The Bible states that Moses never completed the trip. But just before Moses died, God brought him to a mountaintop, where he could look out upon the promised land.

This Bible story had special importance for anyone who loved or admired Martin Luther King. The night before his death, King had referred to the story of Moses. He seemed to sense his destiny as he spoke to a gathering in Memphis. "Like anybody, I would like to live a long life," King said. "Longevity has its place. But I'm not concerned about that now. I just want to do God's will. And he's allowed me to go up to the mountain. And I've looked over, and I've seen the promised land. I may not get there with you. But I want you to know that we as a people will get to the promised land."

Like Moses, Martin Luther King died before his people reached their goal. Abernathy had vowed to carry on in his place. He spoke to the assembled marchers in a gentle, comforting voice that was edged with sorrow. Newspapers across the country printed his words. "I have been to the top of the mountain. I have talked with God about it," Abernathy said. "God told me that Martin did not get there, but you have been so close to Martin I am going to help you get there. If God will lead me, I am going to lead my people into the promised land."

The new president of the Southern Christian Leadership Conference dedicated himself to carrying out the plans that he and King had made. Just weeks after King's death, Abernathy led a Poor People's Campaign, bringing thousands of poor Americans to Washington, D. C. He wanted to show the government and the nation the extent of poverty in the United States. He hoped the campaign would inspire people to take action, to improve living conditions for the poor of every race. He also led demonstrations in Charleston, South Carolina, that resulted in better pay and working conditions for the black hospital workers of that city.

Abernathy faced great challenges during his years of leadership. Many members of the press and the public wanted him to be another Martin Luther King, an expectation that Abernathy considered unrealistic. "No man can fill Dr. King's shoes," he said to reporters.

By the end of the 1960s, the civil rights movement had succeeded in breaking down most of the legal barriers to integration. Abernathy turned to larger social problems, such as poverty, that cross racial lines. Victories became harder to achieve and more difficult to measure.

Also, some African Americans had grown impatient with the nonviolent methods that the Southern Christian Leadership Conference had employed to bring about change, methods such as marches and sit-ins. Young black leaders preached that violence was the only tactic white America would understand.

Throughout his life, Abernathy met every challenge and criticism with the same courage, patience, and inner strength that led to victories during the civil rights years. He remained committed to nonviolence as a way of life.

Ralph David Abernathy dedicated himself to serving God and the people of his race. "Ralph Abernathy was the unsung hero of the civil rights movement," said his longtime colleague Hosea Williams. Abernathy was a tireless worker whose efforts led to important changes in the law, changes that provide protection against discrimination. He worked to bring all Americans closer together, to make all Americans more tolerant and understanding of one another.

Chapter / Two

The Barefoot Boy

Ralph Abernathy's grandmother, Ellen Bell, was a midwife in Marengo County, Alabama. She had delivered many children into the world. On March 11, 1926, she helped her daughter give birth to her tenth child.

As Ellen Bell washed the child and wrapped him in a blanket, she sensed that he possessed unusual talents. She predicted that one day his name would be famous throughout the world.

The child's parents sensed his potential, too. They christened him not Ralph, but David, after the biblical king who slew the giant Goliath. They hoped he would possess his namesake's faith and courage. As an adult, Abernathy wrote about the advice his parents gave him while he was growing up. He wrote that his father told him, "David, if you ever see a good fight, get in it—and win." Abernathy was to recall those words when he joined the fight for civil rights.

Linden, Alabama, was a quiet rural community in the middle of Marengo County, where most people earned their living as farmers. One of Linden's largest farms belonged to David's father, William Abernathy, a man most people called W. L. He was a slender, handsome man who followed a strict moral code. Ralph Abernathy would describe him as "very stern, very stern and commanding" in an interview in 1968. W. L. Abernathy worked hard to improve life for his family and for himself. He invested his money in land, a little at a time, until he owned 500 acres. He believed that the way for African Americans to gain opportunity was through prosperity.

Prosperity was a word on many tongues during the 1930s, when David Abernathy was growing up. Having steady work and money in the bank was only a dream for many men and women. The nation was in the midst of the Great Depression, a period of severe economic problems. Thousands of Americans were without jobs. They lacked money to buy food and pay their bills. To keep their spirits up, people told themselves that "prosperity is just around the corner."

African Americans were among those hit hardest by the Depression. They were often the first to be fired or to take a pay cut. Three to four times as many blacks as whites were unemployed in most cities. In some places, black unemployment reached 80 percent. Soup kitchens—set up to feed the unemployed in many cities and towns— frequently closed their doors to blacks.

In their long, white farmhouse, the family of W. L. Abernathy felt protected from the hardships of the Great Depression. Their fields provided vegetables and fruit. They raised cattle, hogs, and chickens and so had plenty of milk, meat, and eggs. They sold their crops of cotton for cash.

The Abernathys were comfortable, but thrifty. When his parents bought David his first suit, they told him it would have to last for several years. Although David was allergic to the suit's wool fabric and broke out in an itchy rash whenever he put it on, he obediently wore the suit on Sundays until it no longer fit.

By working hard and saving, W. L. Abernathy had accumulated more money than most of the whites in Linden. Blacks and whites alike treated his family with respect. W. L. Abernathy was a recognized leader in Linden's African American community. He was on the school board of the local black high school. He was a deacon of the Hopewell Baptist Church. He was the first African American to serve on a grand jury in Marengo County.

David's mother, Louivery Abernathy, was a quiet woman who was devoted to her family and to God. In contrast to her husband's sternness, she expressed gentleness and kindness. Through her example rather than her words, she taught her children important lessons about love and responsibility.

David learned one of those lessons when he was six years old and about to start school. Because he lived in a large family, David was used to wearing hand-me-down clothing and playing with secondhand toys. But when he went to school, he wanted brand-new books, books not worn from use by an older child. At that time, families in Linden were expected to provide their children's textbooks.

David's father had insisted, though, that he use his brother William's old books. W. L. Abernathy did not want to waste money on new ones. It was a huge letdown for the boy.

David could see that his mother knew how he

felt, and that his disappointment moved her to tears. He was learning a valuable lesson about love. "I believe it was the first time in my life that I understood what love really meant," he wrote in his 1989 autobiography, "that capacity to feel the suffering of others as if it were your own."

Louivery Abernathy seldom stood up to her husband, but she did so on this occasion. When David arrived home after his first day of school, a new set of books was there waiting for him. Right away, he knew who was responsible. He hurried to the kitchen to hug his mother and thank her for her love.

The Abernathys were a religious family who never missed Sunday services. In Sunday school, David learned Bible stories. He absorbed tales of the ancient leaders Moses and Joshua, men who performed miracles and won impossible battles. He heard all about the life of Jesus Christ, whom Christians accept as the Son of God. The story of Jesus carrying his own heavy cross to the site of his Crucifixion impressed David greatly.

Listening to sermons week after week, from the time that he was very young, David grew to admire the pastor of his church, who was an important person in the community. While his sisters made plans to become teachers, David formed career plans of his own. "I knew deep down I would one day end up preaching," he told a *New York Times* reporter in 1968. "I'm a preacher and I love to preach."

Of course, the decision to join the ministry involves more than the desire for respect. It should be based on a strong religious faith, what Abernathy called "the kind of religion that grabs your soul and won't let go." But as a young boy, he had never experienced this kind of religious awakening.

When he was seven years old, his mother told him how to have that experience. She told him to spend a day fasting and praying. You will hear God's voice, she said to her son. One day, David skipped breakfast and went outside to wait to hear from God. He spent hours praying and staring at an old oak tree.

Finally, at three o'clock, he felt what he believed to be God's presence. God spoke to him not with words, Abernathy claimed, but with sensations. "I only know that a sudden peace flooded my soul, and in an instant I was a different human being," he wrote in his autobiography. He had gained the faith that would sustain him for the rest of his life. Then, changed inwardly but still a child, he hurried into the house to eat a plate of cold biscuits.

Farm life meant hard work for everyone in the family. When they were not in school, the older children helped their father in the fields. David, the one who would be different, was assigned the job of helping his mother in the house. "I never farmed," he said to the *New York Times*. "I was always reading and writing, and my father gave up on me early as far as the farm went."

David woke every morning before the sun was up to light a fire in the wood-burning stove, milk the cows, feed the livestock, and collect eggs from the henhouse. He ran errands for his mother later in the day, helped her prepare dinner, and kept an eye on his younger sister and brother, Susie and James Earl.

As a man, Ralph Abernathy liked to call himself "the barefoot boy from Marengo County." He remembered walking along dusty country roads and playing ball with his brothers and sisters in his father's fields. In a big family, there was always someone to play with. Mealtimes were happy occasions as well, times for good food and good company.

When David was 12 years old, one of his sisters had a teacher she admired very much, a man named Ralph David. She started to call her little brother Ralph David, too. The name stuck.

And although some close family members still called him David, to the rest of the world he was Ralph David Abernathy.

Dozens of relatives lived nearby, and as Ralph grew older, he sometimes felt "there was an uncle around every corner, and aunt under every bush." He felt especially close to his father's father, George Abernathy, who had grown up in slavery. When Ralph's grandfather told stories about his slave years, he focused on the pleasant memories, recalling the kindnesses he had received from his white owners. He admitted that many slaves had been treated cruelly, but he refused to be bitter about the past.

Southern slavery ended in 1865, but African Americans had yet to gain the rights and opportunities that whites enjoyed. Following the Civil War, Alabama and the other Southern states had passed their infamous "Jim Crow" laws. Named for an act in 19th-century minstrel shows that ridiculed African Americans, these laws kept blacks apart from white society.

Under Jim Crow, blacks and whites used separate drinking fountains, separate passenger cars on trains, and even separate waiting rooms at railroad and bus stations. Black customers would be turned away from the restaurants, hotels, and barbershops that catered to whites. Black and white children attended different schools. The Jim Crow laws were enforced well into the 20th century.

Looking back on that era for the "Eyes on the Prize" programs, Ralph Abernathy recalled, "You could not use a filling station that was not designated with a restroom for colored. You had a restroom for white males and a restroom for white women, and you had a restroom for colored. Meaning that colored people had to use the same restroom, male and female. And the janitor would never clean up the restroom for the colored people."

In 1896, the Supreme Court had ruled that the Constitution allowed separate services for the races, as long as the facilities for blacks and whites were "separate but equal." But like the rest rooms that Abernathy described, the facilities for African Americans were often inferior.

Growing up, Ralph and his brothers and sisters had little contact with racism and the humiliating Jim Crow laws. They were their own playmates. Their classmates and the members of their church were black. Still, Abernathy recalled in his autobiography, his father warned him not to play with white children. "If you do," W. L. Abernathy said, "every joke will be at your expense. If you wrestle or box with a white child, you will always have to let him win, otherwise he may become aggravated, and that could lead to trouble."

Ralph ran into trouble during childhood only once because of his race. And it resulted from an encounter with an adult, not a child.

Louivery Abernathy had sent him to the local country store for some groceries. One other customer was in the store when he arrived, a white man who was drunk. The man had been sipping a soft drink, which he no longer wanted. He thrust the bottle toward Abernathy and ordered him to drink. Ralph refused. His parents had taught him not to drink from another person's bottle or glass.

The white man, however, expected different behavior. He expected black people to do as they were told by whites. He raised his hand to hit the boy.

It was a dangerous moment. Some Southern whites thought nothing about taking the law into their own hands when dealing with blacks. Violent punishment, from whipping to hanging to burning alive, could be inflicted on blacks who were suspected of wrongdoing. Their alleged crimes ranged from robbery and rape to insulting a white person.

But before the man could strike a blow, the

storekeeper spoke up. Ralph was the son of W. L. Abernathy, he warned. The drunken customer lowered his arm as soon as he heard that name. He was not about to anger such a prominent citizen of Linden.

Young Ralph snatched up his groceries and hurried home.

When Ralph was a teenager, his father suffered a stroke, which is an interruption in the flow of blood to the brain. Although many people survive strokes, W. L. Abernathy had sustained severe brain damage, and he died. Everyone in the family was shocked and saddened, but no one felt the loss more than Ralph's grandfather, George Abernathy. For the rest of his life, Ralph would see, in his memory, the tears on his grandfather's face as he viewed his son's body. He would hear the old man whispering as he was led away, wondering why God had caused him to suffer in this way.

George Abernathy never recovered from the upset caused by his son's death. His own physical and mental health declined rapidly, and in a few years he, too, was dead.

The Abernathys felt the pain of separation again when three of Ralph's brothers left home to serve in World War II. Living on the family farm

Chapter / Three

Taking His Place

Americans in every state followed the news from Europe. In 1939, Germany's Nazi government had seized Czechoslovakia and Poland. Echoing their leader, Adolf Hitler, the Nazis claimed to be part of a "master race," a group that was superior to other people. The Nazis expressed hatred of Jews and other minority groups, and this hatred often erupted in violence.

The American people supported England and France when those countries went to war against Germany. African Americans especially understood the dangers of the ethnic and racial hatred that the Nazis preached.

On December 8, 1941, people in cities and on farms crowded around their radios to listen to President Franklin Roosevelt. "Yesterday, December 7, 1941—a day which will live in infamy—the United States of America was suddenly and deliberately attacked by naval and air forces of the Empire of Japan," Roosevelt told Congress and the nation.

Japanese military planes had attacked the U.S. naval base at Pearl Harbor, Hawaii. The surprise attack had nearly destroyed the American Pacific Fleet. Following the president's speech, Congress voted to declare a state of war between the United States and Japan. Three days later, Germany and its ally, Italy, declared war on the United States.

Americans of all races felt a surge of patriotism. Edgar B. Brown, director of the National Negro Council, informed President Roosevelt, "Twelve million American Negroes renew today their pledge of 100 percent loyalty to their country and our Commander-in-Chief against Japan and all other invaders."

During the war years, between 1941 and 1945, 16 million Americans served in the armed forces. They fought in Europe, the Far East, and North Africa. One million of those men and women were African Americans. The black soldiers entered a segregated, "Jim Crow" army, where they served in separate units from whites but took orders from white officers. At the war's start, there were only 12 black officers in the army. The nation had only one black general, Benjamin O. Davis, Sr.

In spite of the unequal treatment, African Americans made important gains during World War II. They joined the Marine Corps and the Coast Guard for the first time. At the Tuskegee Army Air Field, just 130 miles from Linden, Alabama, the nation's first black fighter pilots received their training. Known as the Tuskegee Airmen, these men proved that African Americans had the courage and intelligence to fly difficult missions in wartime.

At their home in Linden, the Abernathys waited for news from their three members in uniform. Then, in April 1944, another brother was called upon to fight. Ralph received orders to report to Fort Benning, Georgia, America's largest military post, for his army physical. Just three weeks had passed since his 18th birthday.

The bus ride to Fort Benning was Ralph's first trip beyond the borders of Alabama. The rows and rows of marching soldiers at Fort Benning, and the gruff officers barking orders, could easily make a sheltered country boy frightened and nervous. Ralph nearly failed his physical exam because of high blood pressure caused by his nerves. But the army kept him overnight, and when the nurses tested his blood pressure after a good sleep, the reading was normal. A nurse told him he was now a soldier in the U.S. Army.

Ralph went home to Marengo County. As he waited for his orders to report for active duty, he listened to news broadcasts on the progress of the war.

On June 6, 1944, a day remembered as D-day, American and British forces began landing on the coast of Normandy, in northern France. France had been occupied by the Nazis since the early days of the war. By the end of June, 850,000 men and 150,000 tanks, trucks, and jeeps had come ashore on Normandy's beaches. They pushed inland in the months ahead, liberating France and moving toward Germany.

Throughout Europe, the Americans and their allies uncovered the horrors of the Nazi concentration camps. Hitler's forces had rounded up millions of Jews and others who failed to meet their criteria for the "master race." At Auschwitz, Buchenwald, and other death camps, the Nazis systematically starved, tortured, and murdered these people.

Ralph returned to Fort Benning in November to be inducted into the army. He and the other recruits soon found themselves on a train headed north to Fort Devens, Massachusetts, where they would receive their basic training as soldiers.

The Southerners shivered in the cold weather of a New England autumn. Their white commander, Captain Patton, seemed ill at ease with African Americans. Captain Patton came from Maine, a state with a low black population. As they received their training, however, the men would grow to respect Captain Patton for treating them fairly.

The wartime army brought together people from all walks of life. Ralph's new friends included Jack Hatchet, a professional gambler, and Fred Johnson, a quiet man of 35 who accompanied Ralph to church. Private Abernathy felt particularly fond of a young soldier called W. J., who appeared to be mentally retarded. Ralph wondered how W. J. had ever been inducted into the army.

Ralph and the others were busy from sunrise to sundown learning to be infantrymen, or foot soldiers. They practiced shooting their M1 rifles. They learned to protect themselves under gunfire and to survive in the outdoors. Ralph worked especially hard and was one of the four soldiers chosen as platoon sergeants. The promotion brought him respect and authority over a group of men. He might also have to lead the men into combat!

The new soldiers boarded a ship bound for Le Havre, France. The war in Europe was nearly over. Abernathy's unit expected to be part of the "mopping up" operations, the final fighting of the European war.

Traveling through Europe toward the battle lines, the men passed through bombed-out cities where buildings had been reduced to piles of bricks and stones. Everywhere, they saw wounded, suffering people, both enemies and allies. The pain and the destruction of war brought Ralph Abernathy to an important understanding, one that would affect the course of his life. Abernathy relived that decisive moment when writing his autobiography. "I have by now concluded that I am committed in principle to a life of nonviolence," he wrote.

The war in Europe ended before Abernathy's unit saw combat. While the men waited for new orders, two of the soldiers in Abernathy's platoon skipped out on a duty they were to perform.

Patton, who had been promoted to the rank of colonel, ordered that they be punished. The two were to dig a hole six feet deep and six feet across on a rainy night, Patton said. Ralph Abernathy, the platoon sergeant, was to stand watch and see that the order was carried out.

The rain soaked through Ralph's clothes as the night progressed. First he felt chilly, then he felt sick. Finally, he grew weak and passed out. He awoke to find himself in an army hospital, where doctors said he had come down with rheumatic fever, a throat infection that may spread to the joints, heart, and other organs.

Colonel Patton visited Ralph in the hospital to tell him the unit was going to the South Pacific to aid in the fight against Japan. Patton promised that Ralph could join the others when he recovered. Abernathy never made it to the Far East, though. The day after Colonel Patton's visit, Abernathy learned he was being sent home with the wounded.

Many years later, Abernathy would be stunned to find out that he and one other soldier were the only members of his unit to survive the war. Jack Hatchet, Fred Johnson, W. J., Colonel Patton, and all of the rest died in a battle against Japan.

Home in Alabama, Ralph enjoyed his

mother's good, rich cooking. He gained back the weight he had lost while ill. He regained his strength under his mother's loving care. When World War II ended, Ralph's brothers were among the millions of veterans who returned home alive and well.

The U.S. government offered several programs to help the war veterans resume their civilian lives. For example, former soldiers and sailors could receive government funds to attend college. Ralph took advantage of this program and enrolled in Alabama State University in the state capital, Montgomery.

Founded in 1867 in the town of Marion, Alabama, the college was originally called the Lincoln School, after President Abraham Lincoln. It purpose then was to train black teachers. The whites of Marion burned the school in 1887 and refused to let the black community rebuild it. The students and faculty began meeting in a Montgomery church building. With time, donations of land and money, and funds from the state of Alabama, the school grew into a university for African Americans.

Abernathy adapted easily to college life. Living in a men's dormitory reminded him of being in the army. Studying for his classes was like preparing to become platoon sergeant. Abernathy earned high grades, and he took part in extracurricular activities. He starred in the school play during his sophomore year of college. He was active in student government.

The professors at Alabama State often spoke to their students about the problems African Americans faced in the United States. One of Abernathy's teachers stressed the importance of voting rights. Like other Southern states, Alabama made it difficult for blacks to register to vote. Black men and women who tried to register were given literacy tests that were nearly impossible to pass. Registration offices were open at hours when many blacks would be at work. Finally, the whites in some communities used threats to keep African Americans from registering.

Abernathy's professor explained that voting would enable blacks to elect officials who would provide them with needed public services, from garbage collection to improved schools. Eventually, blacks themselves might even be elected to office. The talk filled Abernathy with civic spirit, and he convinced several students to accompany him to Montgomery's courthouse. They were going to register to vote.

A white woman working at the courthouse

Black citizens filling out voter registration forms in Mississippi

handed the students a four-page literacy test. Most of the young men completed the test quickly. The woman looked over their papers and told them they had failed. They had left some of the answers blank, she said.

Abernathy, who was still working on his test, made sure he answered every question, even if he only wrote that the question did not apply to him. He suspected the woman did not know the correct answers herself. And when she saw that he had responded to every question, she had no choice but to say he had passed.

Then the woman told Abernathy to do one more thing. She told him to recite, word for word, the Thirteenth Amendment to the Constitution.

Abernathy did not know the words to this amendment, but, he guessed, neither did the woman. Confidently, he recited the Pledge of Allegiance. It turned out that Abernathy's guess had been correct. He left the courthouse with a brand-new voter registration card.

College gave Abernathy his first opportunities to plan protests. As a student council member, he organized a hunger strike to protest the poor-quality food served in the Alabama State dining hall. Later, as president of the junior class, he led a group of students to the college president's office to demand better housing for the male students. The men were living in army barracks left over from the war. They had to put up with broken plumbing, no heat, and cracked walls.

In both cases, the college responded to the protesters' demands. Abernathy learned a lesson that would give him the courage to stand up to government officials during civil rights protests later on. "You can deal with the most awesome authority on an equal basis if the people are on your side," he wrote in his autobiography.

Religion remained important in Ralph Abernathy's life. Friends and family members asked him when he planned to announce his calling. It is a common practice in some religious denominations for young people who feel called to the ministry to stand up and announce this fact in church. Ralph had talked about being a preacher since early childhood. Yet he did not feel ready, he said, to make a public statement.

At this time in his life, Ralph met a young woman he liked very much, Juanita Odessa Jones. Juanita wanted to be a teacher. She was planning to enter Tennessee State University in Nashville. Ralph admired her quick mind and strong character. Juanita claimed she would never be a preacher's wife, but that did not stop the two from spending time together. Both Ralph and Juanita claimed to be uninterested in marriage.

College friendships could never be more important than family for Ralph Abernathy. He looked forward to summers and holidays, when he returned to the farm in Linden and many welcoming, familiar faces.

Ralph's happiness when he traveled home for Thanksgiving in 1947 was clouded by the fact that his mother was ill. For some time, Louivery Abernathy had suffered from rheumatoid arthritis, a painful inflammation of the joints. The family had watched her grow weaker over the past several months. She was under a doctor's care, but there seemed to be little the doctor could do.

On Sunday, the last day of Ralph's visit, his mother stayed home from church. This was something she had never done. Ralph, his brothers, and his sisters were clearly worried. Before he returned to college that afternoon, Ralph went to his mother's room. He wrapped her in his arms, never wanting to let go. Two days later, he learned that his mother had died. He hurried back to Linden, where his family had gathered once more.

Ralph's grief overwhelmed him. His childhood home was filled with fond memories and loving relatives, but they offered no comfort. He went outdoors and stood in the cold November night, feeling more alone than he had ever felt before.

The next day was filled with planning for the funeral. As the brothers selected a casket and the sisters chose a dress for their mother to wear, they turned to Ralph for advice. Although he was younger than most of them, they now looked upon him as the head of the family.

Ralph thought about Juanita Jones, who was at school in Nashville, during this difficult time. He sent her a telegram to tell her of his loss. But when days and weeks passed and he received no reply from her, he decided that their friendship must be over.

The pair saw each other at Christmastime.

Juanita explained that Ralph's telegram had been greatly delayed, and that she had wanted to express her sympathy in person. Ralph felt relieved to hear Juanita's explanation, but it seemed that his affection for her was gone.

More and more, the church occupied his thoughts. The war had taught him to choose a life of nonviolence. He had earned the respect of his peers and his family. The time had come to take his place in the world. Ralph David Abernathy felt ready to dedicate his life to God's work. On Mother's Day, 1948, he stood up in the Hopewell Baptist Church. He wrote about that special Sunday in his memoirs. On that day, he told the congregation of family and friends, "I want to announce my call to the ministry of Jesus Christ."

Chapter / Four

God's Plan

Ralph David Abernathy graduated from Alabama State University in the spring of 1950 with a degree in mathematics. The next fall, he enrolled in Atlanta University, in the capital of Georgia, to continue his education. He would always have a flair for the abstract thinking that mathematics requires. But he chose to earn his master's degree in sociology, the study of human society and social problems. Abernathy told an interviewer in 1968 that as a budding preacher, "I realized my life was with people."

On Sundays during the school year, local churches invited him to be a guest preacher, to practice writing and delivering sermons. Sometimes he listened to other young preachers. Abernathy attended Atlanta's Ebenezer Baptist Church one Sunday to hear a guest preacher, a man who, like himself, was still a student. That young man was Martin Luther King, Jr. Abernathy heard a preacher who seemed learned, self-assured, and inspiring. Right away, Abernathy said, he knew King was an outstanding man.

Abernathy and King ran into each other several times in Atlanta, but they made no effort to become friends. Another relationship occupied Ralph's thoughts. It was his romance with Juanita Jones.

Ralph had returned to his old college, Alabama State, for the homecoming weekend in November 1950. He attended the Thanksgiving Day football game and visited with his old classmates. He also called on Juanita, who was home from college for the holiday. Ralph took Juanita out to dinner and felt his old affection for her return. In fact, his feelings were stronger than they were before.

Juanita cared for Ralph, too. She decided she could be a preacher's wife after all. The pair promised that one day they would marry.

Ralph Abernathy finished the work on his

master's degree after one year of study. He then had a choice to make. Should he earn still another degree, in theology, the study of religion? Or should he take a job as dean of men at Alabama State University?

Abernathy hoped to be a religious scholar before becoming a full-time minister. But the job offer tempted him. He could earn some money before starting back to school. As dean of men, he would keep order in the male students' dormitories. He would counsel students with problems, just as a caring pastor would.

There was another reason for choosing Montgomery. He had the chance to be a part-time pastor for a small church. The Eastern Star Baptist Church was located in Demopolis, Alabama, close to Abernathy's hometown of Linden. Its congregation had asked him to preach there on Sundays.

An older pastor, a man who had befriended Abernathy in Atlanta, warned him not to take the job. If he did, the older man said, he probably never would go back to school. Marriage, children, and life's responsibilities would soon keep him too busy.

The pastor's warning proved to be correct. Ralph Abernathy took the job at Alabama State and never returned to school. Yet years later, he knew he had made the right choice. Like many religious people, he felt the hand of God guiding his life. "The Good Lord had other plans for me," he wrote in his autobiography. "He wanted me to be in Montgomery during those years."

In early 1952, when he was 26 years old, Abernathy had a new job opportunity. The people of the First Baptist Church, a historic 100-year-old church in the city of Montgomery, asked him to be their pastor. Abernathy accepted the offer, and church duties filled his days. He wrote sermons and preached on Sundays. He presided at weddings, baptisms, and funerals. He visited the sick and the aged, counseled troubled people, and led Wednesday-night prayer meetings.

Abernathy felt settled at the First Baptist Church and ready to share his home with a wife. He and Juanita married on August 13, 1952, and, months later, the couple had another reason to rejoice. Juanita told Ralph she was expecting a baby.

The child was a boy. Ralph, Juanita, their relatives, and the members of the First Baptist Church welcomed tiny Ralph David Abernathy, Jr., into the world. At the same time, they worried. The baby was ill. The infant's pediatrician assured the concerned parents that he probably would get well. But the illness worsened, and the baby died.

Ralph and Juanita Abernathy in 1968

Ralph and Juanita Abernathy had had little time to get to know their son, yet they already loved him dearly. Their sorrow was enormous. More than 30 years later, they still felt the pain of this loss from time to time. Ralph David Abernathy, Jr., was buried in a cemetery across the street from the First Baptist Church.

In time, Juanita became pregnant again. She gave birth to a healthy daughter, a child the Abernathys named Juandalynn. Caring for Juandalynn and watching her grow eased the sadness that Ralph and Juanita had felt for so long. Thanks to Juandalynn, they felt happiness again.

The Abernathys also found joy in the company of friends. Guests often stopped by to share meals and conversation. One evening, the couple invited a young man to stay for dinner. He was being considered for the job of pastor at Montgomery's Dexter Avenue Baptist Church. Ralph Abernathy had met the young man before, in Atlanta. He was Martin Luther King, Jr.

King was offered the position, and he and his wife, Coretta, settled in Montgomery. The Kings and the Abernathys enjoyed one another's company. Night after night, they ate dinner together. Juanita and Coretta took turns cooking.

The Abernathys and the Kings got to know one another very well. They discussed the issues of the day and their deeply held beliefs. In the years ahead, Abernathy would see his friendship with King as part of a divine plan. "God made us good friends so that he could later make us a working team," he explained in an interview.

There was so much to talk about that conversations lasted long into the night. Changes had been taking place, changes that promised new opportunities for African Americans.

President Harry S. Truman had ended segregation in the U.S. armed forces in 1948. The president had also appointed committees, composed of blacks and whites, to look into racial problems. What's more, nine states and eight cities had forbidden discrimination in public housing.

On May 17, 1954, the Supreme Court of the United States had ruled that segregated schools violated the rights of African American children. Parents in Kansas, Delaware, Washington, D.C., and elsewhere had taken their local school boards to court. The parents claimed that by attending separate schools—schools for black students only—their children received a poorer education than white children did.

The schools for blacks often lacked modern textbooks and supplies. Some children traveled long distances to reach the black schools, even though there were other schools, exclusively for white children, in their own neighborhoods. Segregation made the children feel they were less than equal as human beings.

The local judges who heard these cases ruled in favor of the school boards. Segregated schools, they said, were in keeping with the 1896 Supreme Court decision that allowed "separate but equal" facilities for the races.

The Supreme Court, however, was ready to look at the issue of segregation again. The Court's nine justices agreed to review the cases of the parents who had sued their school boards. They grouped the cases under the name *Brown v. the Board of Education*. Oliver Brown was a father in Topeka, Kansas, who had sued his local schools.

In announcing the Court's decision, Chief Justice Earl Warren said, "We conclude, unanimously, that in the field of public education, the doctrine of 'separate but equal' has no place. Separate educational facilities are inherently unequal."

The Abernathys and the Kings had been excited by the Supreme Court decision. Still, they worried about the racial discrimination that existed throughout the United States and especially in the South. They understood that Southern communities would resist complying with the new Supreme Court ruling. Change would require pressure from African American leaders and maybe from the federal government as well.

Still, the ruling marked the beginning of the end of legal segregation in the United States. It was the first step toward ending the indignity that Montgomery's black residents endured every day, whether they wanted to buy a hamburger for lunch or ride the city's buses.

City law required African Americans to enter a bus at the front, deposit their fare in the coin box next to the driver, then get off the bus and enter again at the rear. An imaginary line separated the seats for whites, in the front of the bus, from the seats for blacks, in the back. Black passengers had to obey the driver's orders about where to sit. If the driver wanted them to give up their seats so that white passengers could sit down, the blacks had to comply. Those who refused to obey risked going to jail.

African Americans often endured insults and abuse from the white bus drivers. One driver used the metal coin box to beat a black passenger, a man who was ill and under a doctor's care, because of a disagreement.

Sadly, violence against African Americans was all too common in the South. In the summer of 1955, the nation was shocked by the murder of Emmett Till, a black teenager from Chicago who went to visit his cousins in Mississippi. Ignorant of the way blacks were expected to address whites in the South, Till casually called out, "Bye, Baby," to a white cashier in a country store. Emmett Till's body was found several days later, floating in a river. The cashier's husband and another man had beaten the boy and shot him in the head. Defending these actions, one of the murderers told a journalist that Till had thought himself equal to a white person.

Abernathy and King understood that any African American who worked openly for change in the South could be the target of violent acts. They talked about strategies for improving life in Montgomery, nonviolent methods that would be in contrast to the brutality of segregation. Both men had studied the writings of the American author Henry David Thoreau and the teachings of the Indian leader Mohandas Gandhi. They had found much to inspire and guide them.

Thoreau, a resident of Concord, Massachusetts, in the 19th century, had favored a form of protest known as civil disobedience. "Unjust laws exist," Thoreau wrote in a famous essay, "On the Duty of Civil Disobedience." He believed that people who followed their conscience had a duty to disobey those laws. "What I have to do is to see, at any rate, that I do not lend myself to the wrong which I condemn," Thoreau went on to explain. The law Thoreau found unjust required him to pay

*Ralph Abernathy with Martin Luther King, Jr., in
Montgomery, Alabama*

taxes to support a war with Mexico that he
believed to be wrong. A century later, the Jim
Crow laws troubled Abernathy and King.

Gandhi, who led India to independence in a
peaceful revolution, published several collections
of his writings. In them, he claimed that civil
disobedience was "the highest duty of a citizen."
In addition, he stressed that a protest must be
nonviolent if it is to bring about lasting good.

"I am an uncompromising opponent of violent
methods even to serve the noblest of causes,"
Mohandas Gandhi had stated. "Experience
convinces me that permanent good can never be

the outcome of untruth and violence."

According to Gandhi, the nonviolent person must try to love his or her enemy, to work patiently to change the enemy's understanding. "The appeal is never to his fear; it is, must be, always to his heart," Gandhi taught.

Abernathy and King, like Gandhi, considered it the duty of religious people to work to solve social problems. "Those who say that religion has nothing to do with politics do not know what religion means," Gandhi taught. As Christian ministers, Abernathy and King preached a "social gospel." To them, following Christian teachings meant taking a stand on issues they believed to be wrong.

The two ministers assumed, though, that any nonviolent action they might take to gain opportunities for Montgomery's blacks would occur at some distant time.

Then, in December 1955, Abernathy received a telephone call from E. D. Nixon, a man well-known in Montgomery who had worked on behalf of his fellow black citizens. He was a man Abernathy knew and admired. Nixon explained that Rosa Parks, a seamstress in a downtown department store, had been arrested on a Montgomery bus. Parks, who also worked with the

National Association for the Advancement of Colored People (NAACP), had refused to give up her seat to a white passenger. The time had come, Nixon said, for Montgomery's blacks to protest their treatment on the city's buses.

Nixon worked as a Pullman porter on railroad trains. His work was going to take him away from Montgomery for several days. He asked Abernathy to organize the public response.

Abernathy agreed without a moment's hesitation to take on the task. "Let me know what you want me to do," he said.

Rosa Parks on a Montgomery, Alabama, bus in December 1956

Chapter / Five

Walk Together Children

Rosa Parks was eager to get home when she boarded a Montgomery city bus on December 1, 1955. After a long day's work at the Montgomery Fair department store, the 42-year-old Parks was tired. It felt good to sit down, relax, and rest her sore shoulder.

The bus picked up more passengers as it traveled its route. Soon, every seat at the front of the bus was taken. When a white man climbed aboard and had nowhere to sit, the driver ordered the four riders in Rosa Parks's row to get up. They were the African Americans closest to the front. The driver wanted the four black passengers to give up their seats so that one white passenger could sit down.

The two women sitting across the aisle from Parks stood up and moved. The man next to her left his seat, too. But Rosa Parks stayed where she was. The driver repeated his command and threatened to call the police unless she obeyed. Parks dared him to do so. She was not about to move.

It wasn't tiredness that kept Rosa Parks in her seat. Complying with the driver's order would have been the easier thing to do. Rather, Parks refused to cooperate with a system that treated her people so poorly. She was motivated by the same love of freedom that prompted her to work with the NAACP.

The driver left the bus and telephoned the police. He quickly returned with two white patrolmen, who asked the determined passenger why she would not move. Parks responded with a question of her own: "Why do you push us around?"

The police arrested Rosa Parks and took her off to jail. "I was well aware of what could happen or what might happen to me, other than just being arrested," Parks recalled. No violence occurred, however. The police fingerprinted Parks and sent her home. Her court appearance was scheduled for the next Monday.

After relating these events to Abernathy on

the telephone, E. D. Nixon asked him to organize a boycott of the city buses for that Monday. Some 25,000 African Americans were regular riders of the city buses. They provided three-fourths of the bus company's earnings. By boycotting buses, even for one day, the city's blacks would demonstrate their strength and disapproval. They would also cost the city money.

Abernathy immediately contacted all of the black ministers in Montgomery, informing them of a meeting that night at King's Dexter Avenue Baptist Church. Teachers, lawyers, doctors, business leaders, and others attended the meeting as well. Everyone was upset over Rosa Parks's arrest. Everyone favored the boycott. They agreed to spread the word to the rest of the black community.

Jo Ann Robinson, a professor of English at Alabama State, printed hundreds of fliers to be passed out throughout the city. "Don't ride the buses to work, to town, to school or anywhere on Monday," the fliers read. "You can afford to stay out of school for one day if you have no other way to go except by bus. You can also afford to stay out of town for one day. If you work, take a cab or walk. But please, children and grown-ups, don't ride the bus at all on Monday."

On Sunday morning, preachers spoke about

the boycott during their sermons. Congregations sang spirituals that inspired them to sacrifice the convenience of the buses for the cause of equality. "Walk together children, don't get weary," go the words to one spiritual. "There's going to be a great camp meeting in the promised land."

Abernathy and King visited the local bars and pool halls to spread the news of the protest there.

The white community learned about the boycott, too. That Sunday, an article appeared in the *Montgomery Advertiser,* a local newspaper, describing the black residents' plans. The article, intended to inform white Montgomery, helped to inform black Montgomery as well. "We couldn't have paid for the publicity the white folks gave us free of charge," Abernathy commented.

Monday morning, December 5, was a time of nervous excitement for Ralph and Juanita Abernathy. Would people stay off the buses, the Abernathys wondered, as they had been asked to do? Would the boycott succeed or fail? Together with King, Ralph and Juanita watched from the front window of their house as a bus came down the street. Usually filled with black passengers at that hour, the bus was empty. "For the first time in the history of Montgomery, blacks were acting together to resist racial injustice," Ralph

Abernathy recalled in his autobiography. "It was indeed a new day." King insisted that a miracle had taken place.

People walked to work that morning, hitched rides, pedaled bicycles, and traveled in old, dented pickup trucks. Some workers arrived at their jobs on mules. Others rode in old-fashioned horse-drawn buggies. Black soldiers stationed at nearby military posts gave rides to people in their free time.

The police followed several buses along their routes, thinking that some African Americans might try to frighten others out of boarding a bus. Yet it was the sight of the police cars that kept a few would-be riders away!

Seeing the empty buses caused the boycotters to feel proud of themselves as the hours passed, to cheer, tell jokes, and laugh. But for Ralph Abernathy and the other boycott leaders, there was much to be done. In the morning, they attended Rosa Parks's court hearing. They listened as the judge found her guilty of breaking the city's segregation law and fined her $10. In the afternoon, they got together to decide the future course of the protest.

The city's black population had shown strength, cooperation, and a commitment to change. All of the leaders wanted the boycott to continue. They decided to form an organization to guide their actions in the days ahead. Abernathy suggested the organization's name, the Montgomery Improvement Association. Rufus Lewis, a local businessman, nominated King to be its president.

The nomination took King and Abernathy by surprise. Both had expected the president to be someone older. King was new to Montgomery and not well-known. The group agreed to have King as their president, though, and the 26-year-old minister accepted the post.

The group also compiled a list of demands about how black people were to be treated on the buses. "Our first demand was to have more courtesy on the part of the bus drivers, to eliminate them calling our women names," Abernathy said during an interview in the 1970s. The group demanded changes in the rules governing seating, so that no black passenger would have to give up a seat to a white person, or ride standing up when there were empty seats. The final demand was for black drivers on bus routes used mostly by black passengers.

A public meeting was scheduled for that evening, to inform the black population about the continuing boycott plans. Abernathy and King wondered whether many people would show up.

They arrived at the Holt Street Baptist Church, where the meeting was to be held, to discover every seat filled and a crowd spilling out onto the sidewalk.

The crowd cheered loudly as the two young ministers entered the church. The people were proud of themselves and proud of what they had achieved.

The meeting began with a hymn, a reading from the Scriptures, and a prayer. Then Abernathy introduced King to the audience. It was the first time many in the church heard King speak. His words flowed with grace and force.

King reviewed the events of Rosa Parks's arrest and of the day's boycott. He expressed his hope for a society based on justice and equality. To create that society, he cautioned, black Americans would have to face insults, injury, and sometimes even death.

Carefully, King explained the concept of nonviolent protest. He summed up the ideas of Gandhi and Thoreau. He urged the boycotters to meet racist attacks with patience and persuasion. If they did so, King predicted, "when the history books are written in future generations, the historians will have to pause and say, 'There lived a great people—a black people—who injected new meaning and dignity into the veins of civilization.' This is our challenge and our overwhelming responsibility."

When the applause died down, Abernathy stood before the crowd. He read the list of demands that had been prepared—demands for courtesy, fair seating, and black drivers. Then he called for a vote, asking people to stand if they wanted the boycott to continue. Within moments, everyone in the church was standing. They could hear the cheers of those gathered outside. Abernathy surveyed the scene with joy. "The fear left that had shackled us across the years—all left suddenly when we were in that church together," he said in the "Eyes on the Prize" series.

That night, King and Abernathy established a pattern that would work well for them at countless gatherings in the years ahead. King spoke first, presenting the movement's goals and philosophy. Abernathy then translated those ideas into practical terms. It was his job to inspire people and to outline strategies for the coming protest.

"As a speaker, he was persuasive and dynamic, with the gift of laughing people into positive action," King wrote about Abernathy in *Stride Toward Freedom*. "The people loved and respected him as a symbol of courage and strength."

The Reverend Abernathy addresses a group in his persuasive and dynamic manner.

Abernathy and the other leaders expected the boycott to last a few more days, but the black people of Montgomery surprised them. They were willing to accept hardship, for as long as it would take, to achieve their goals.

People continued to pitch in and help one another. The city's 18 black-owned taxicab companies agreed to charge black passengers the standard bus fare, 10 cents, instead of the minimal rate for taxis, 45 cents. Men and women who owned cars gave rides to others.

Time magazine reported that one of Montgomery's ministers offered a ride to an older woman who was walking along the road. "Sister, aren't you getting tired?" the minister asked. "My soul has been tired for a long time," the woman replied. "Now my feet are tired, and my soul is resting."

"One feels history is being made in Montgomery these days," wrote a white reader in a letter to the *Montgomery Advertiser.* "It is hard to imagine a soul so dead, a heart so hard, a vision so blinded and provincial as not to be awed with admiration at the quiet dignity, discipline and dedication with which the Negroes have conducted the boycott."

Accounts of the boycott appeared in newspapers throughout the country. The Montgomery Improvement Association began to receive contributions of money from black and white Americans who supported their efforts. They used the funds to buy a fleet of station wagons, nicknamed "rolling churches." They organized car pools to transport people to their destinations.

On Mondays and Thursdays, the association held "pep" meetings to encourage people to stick with the boycott. Old film footage shows Abernathy speaking from a church pulpit at one of those meetings. "Not only is this the show of

Negroes in Montgomery, but this is the show of Negroes all over America," Abernathy said in that speech. "And then I want to go a little further than that and tell you that, truly, this show is the show of all freedom-loving people all over the world."

On Fridays and Saturdays, Abernathy and King offered workshops in nonviolence. They taught the protesters ways to respond in case of assault, methods to use instead of fighting back. The men and women attending these workshops learned to respond to verbal taunts and insults with quotes from the Bible. They practiced guarding their heads and bodies against physical attack. They learned to fold their hands over their heads to protect their skulls. Bringing the elbows together in front of the eyes would prevent injury to the face. The participants learned how to fold up their bodies to protect their internal organs.

Abernathy and King also taught the participants to relax their muscles and let their bodies go limp if they were arrested. This response would make it difficult for the police to handle them.

With the bus company losing money every day, tempers were short among the city's white leaders. "We have pussyfooted around on this boycott long enough," stated Mayor W. A. Gayle, according to *Time* magazine. "The Negroes are laughing at white people behind their backs." Gayle's government threatened to fine the black-owned taxi companies for charging less than the minimal fare.

Other threats were more ominous. On January 30, a bomb exploded on the porch of King's home. Two days later, Nixon's house was bombed. No one was injured and little damage was done, but the danger of violence was indeed very real.

The city officials dredged up an old law forbidding boycotts in certain labor disputes. They contended that the bus boycotters were breaking this law. A grand jury called for the arrest of 115 black leaders—ministers, businesspeople, lawyers, and doctors. "In this state, we are committed to segregation by custom and by law," the grand jury's indictment read. "We intend to maintain it."

One of the first to be arrested was the Reverend Ralph David Abernathy. The police came to his door on February 22, George Washington's Birthday, to escort him to jail. Abernathy had been raised to respect the law nearly as much as he respected God. He was glad his parents could not see him being arrested.

Those arrested were thankful merely to be fingerprinted, to have their pictures taken, and to be released on $300 bond. During his years in the civil rights movement, Abernathy would be arrested many more times. He would spend many days and nights in jail. He would be treated well sometimes, and poorly at other times.

If the Washington's birthday arrests were intended to scare the black community and end the protest, they failed in their purpose. The Montgomery bus boycott lasted through the chilly days of winter and the heat of an Alabama summer.

Acting together, several African Americans filed a suit in federal court against the city of Montgomery. They claimed the bus segregation laws violated the Fourteenth Amendment to the Constitution, which protected citizens against laws that took away their rights.

The court decided the case in favor of the African Americans. Lawyers for the city of Montgomery then appealed to the United States Supreme Court, hoping to have the decision reversed. However, on November 14, 1956, the Supreme Court declined to review the case. The decision of the lower court would stand. This meant that discrimination on public transportation was illegal in Montgomery and anywhere else in the United States. Passengers of all races were free to sit in any seat they chose.

The next night, 8,000 people gathered at two churches to celebrate their victory. It was a victory far greater than had seemed possible 11 months earlier, when the boycott began.

At one of the churches, the crowd interrupted a Lutheran minister's reading of the Scriptures to cheer and clap their hands. A newspaper reporter asked Ralph Abernathy if this behavior seemed peculiar.

"Yes it is," Abernathy responded to the reporter. "Just as it is peculiar for people to walk in the snow and rain when there are empty buses available; just as it is peculiar for people to pray for those who persecute them; just as it is peculiar for the Southern Negro to stand up and look a white man in the face as an equal."

Chapter / Six

Keep Moving, Birmingham!

The Montgomery bus boycott continued for 37 more days, until the Supreme Court mandate— the official order to end bus segregation—reached the city.

On December 21, 1956, Ralph Abernathy rode the first integrated bus to travel the streets of Montgomery, Alabama. He smiled for the news cameras, but he remained alert for trouble. He feared some whites might respond to integration with violence.

A leader of the White Citizens Council, a racist organization, had warned in a public statement, "Any attempt to enforce this decision will lead to riot and bloodshed." The city commission had resolved at a meeting to "do all in its power to oppose the integration of the Negro race with the white race in Montgomery."

The violence started a week later. Snipers began firing guns at buses carrying African Americans. One bullet hit a pregnant black woman in the leg. It became necessary to shut down the bus system after 5:00 P.M. to protect the public.

Many of the people who had stayed off the buses for a year to protest inequality now stayed off for safety. However, their accomplishment had been a great one. Abernathy and King, inspired by the boycott's success, contacted ministers from other Southern cities. They talked about forming a larger organization to work on behalf of African Americans.

They scheduled a meeting with the other ministers in Atlanta. On January 9, 1957, Abernathy traveled to Atlanta with Coretta and Martin Luther King. Juanita, who was pregnant, stayed in Montgomery with Juandalynn.

Ralph was sleeping at the home of King's parents that night when the sound of the telephone awakened him. King's father knocked on his bedroom door to say that Juanita was on the line. She was calling with bad news. Their home had been bombed.

Juanita told Ralph that the bomb had exploded on the porch, just outside the room where she and Juandalynn slept. They had not been hurt, but the room's outer wall had been blasted away. If the bomb had gone off a few inches to the right, a firefighter advised, it would have ignited the gas line going into the house. The whole house would have been blown to pieces and anyone inside would have been killed.

Ralph immediately packed to return to Montgomery, and King insisted on going with him. Coretta King offered to stay in Atlanta and conduct the meeting. Ralph called Juanita back to let her know his plans. As the couple spoke, several more bomb explosions were heard in Montgomery. A white policeman coldly informed Juanita that one of the bombs had damaged Abernathy's First Baptist Church.

Ralph Abernathy rushed home to Montgomery to see for himself that his family was all right and to hold them in his arms. Then he went to see what had happened to his church.

A sign reading "condemned" had been nailed to the front of the once-beautiful church. Several of its stained glass windows had been shattered.

Abernathy's wife and daughter barely escaped harm when a bomb exploded outside their home on January 9, 1957.

Shards of colored glass littered the ground. The entire building leaned to one side.

Abernathy blamed himself and his role in the boycott for the explosion. The stress and guilt that he felt made him physically ill. His congregation, however, helped their distressed pastor feel better. The men and women of the First Baptist Church voiced their support of his work for civil rights. They vowed to rebuild their damaged church.

The bombings revealed to Abernathy the depth of the fear and hatred that lay behind segregation. He now realized, as he wrote in his autobiography, that "when evil is defeated, when there is nothing left to win, only then does its true nature reveal itself."

As work on the church progressed, the new organization of black leaders took shape. It was called the Southern Christian Leadership Conference and had members from 11 states. King was elected its president, and Abernathy its secretary-treasurer. The organization dedicated itself to nonviolent work for racial equality.

In 1957, King moved to Atlanta to be pastor of the Ebenezer Baptist Church. He urged Abernathy to come along, to continue their friendship and their work together. The Abernathys resisted at first. They had started to put down roots in Montgomery. They had a second daughter, Donzaleigh, and soon there would be a third child, Ralph David Abernathy III. But when Ralph Abernathy was called to the pulpit of Atlanta's West Hunter Street Baptist Church, the family decided to move.

In Atlanta and other American cities, people talked about changes occurring in the field of civil rights. The success of the Montgomery bus boycott encouraged many African Americans to protest injustice in their communities.

The blacks of Tallahassee, Florida, boycotted
their buses to force their city to comply with the
Supreme Court mandate. In Greensboro, North
Carolina, black college students staged sit-ins at
lunch counters where they had been refused
service because of their race. They remained
seated at the lunch counters until closing time.
Soon, sit-ins were occurring throughout the
South.

Protesters called Freedom Riders broke down
racial barriers on interstate bus routes. Although
they employed a nonviolent tactic, riding in
racially mixed groups, many Freedom Riders
received vicious beatings from angry mobs. On
Mother's Day, 1961, a crowd of whites in
Birmingham, Alabama, attacked some Freedom
Riders while the police stood by and did nothing.

The Southern Christian Leadership
Conference worked for racial equality in such
places as Albany, Georgia, where boycotters drove
the bus company out of business. One of its best-
known and most successful campaigns took place
in Birmingham, in the spring of 1963.

Many African Americans called Birmingham
the "worst city in the U.S.A." This industrial city
of 350,000 had a reputation for racial hatred.
Some members of the police and fire departments

Black college students staged sit-ins at lunch counters where they had been refused service.

had ties to the Ku Klux Klan, a racist organization known for violence against African Americans.

Public officials such as Police Commissioner "Bull" Connor encouraged cruel treatment of the city's blacks. Between 1957 and 1963, 18 bombs exploded in Birmingham's black neighborhoods. The city closed its parks, pools, and golf courses rather than allow blacks to enjoy them.

Connor's remarks showed him to be a fearful man who mistrusted anyone different from himself. Sitting before news cameras, he said, "The so-called Negro movement is a part of the attempted takeover of our country by the lazy, the indolent, the beatniks, the ignorant, and by some misguided religions and bleeding hearts."

Inspired by the successes of the civil rights movement in other places, the African Americans of Birmingham wanted to integrate their city's downtown shopping area. The Reverend Fred Shuttlesworth of Birmingham had led demonstrations calling for integrated lunch counters, drinking fountains, and department store fitting rooms, as well as the hiring of black salespeople.

Shuttlesworth asked the Southern Christian Leadership Conference for help. He recalled his words for the the "Eyes on the Prize" series. "Birmingham is where it's at, gentlemen," Shuttlesworth remembered telling Abernathy and his associates. "As Birmingham goes, so goes the nation."

Abernathy and King arrived in Birmingham in early April. They set up their headquarters in the Gaston Motel, owned by a black millionaire. They arranged to hold public meetings in the Sixteenth Street Baptist Church. They called their planned protest Project C, for "confrontation." They knew that if they confronted white Birmingham, Bull Connor would respond harshly and violently. People might be injured or even killed. But Connor could actually further civil rights by showing the nation the true cruelty of racism and the rightness of the African Americans' cause.

Easter Sunday was approaching as Project C began. Because many people liked to buy new clothes for this holiday, Birmingham's merchants usually did a brisk business in the weeks before Easter. The protest leaders planned a boycott of the downtown stores, to disrupt business at this busy time and to pressure the merchants to meet their demands.

On the first day of protests, several lunch counters closed to avoid sit-ins. Bull Connor's police force arrested 20 blacks for picketing downtown stores. On Saturday, April 6, Fred Shuttlesworth led 30 marchers to Birmingham City Hall. They, too, went to jail.

But the Birmingham campaign was just beginning. Abernathy compared the continuing marches and protests to the plagues that Moses and his brother, Aaron, created in Egypt. According to the Bible story Abernathy knew so well, Moses and Aaron used God-given power to convince the pharaoh of Egypt to free the Hebrew people, who were imprisoned in Egypt as slaves. Moses and Aaron caused the Egyptians to endure plagues of fire, hailstones, locusts, boils, and more.

"Old Pharaoh didn't believe Moses and

Aaron—not until they had unleashed ten plagues on Egypt," Abernathy said in his autobiography. "We figured there would have to be more plagues for Birmingham, particularly as long as Bull Connor was in power."

The next day, as the protesters continued to plague Birmingham peacefully, Connor began to reveal the full force of the power he was willing to wield. It was Palm Sunday, one week before Easter. A. D. King, Martin Luther King's brother, led a prayer march into downtown Birmingham. Connor ordered the police to use nightsticks and dogs to break up the march. News photographers captured images that shocked the nation, images of police dogs tearing at marchers' clothes.

Connor also sought an injunction, a court order banning any more marches from taking place. The court order listed 133 civil rights leaders by name, forbidding them from taking part in any demonstrations and from encouraging others to protest. The names of Ralph David Abernathy and Martin Luther King were high on that list.

The police hid microphones wherever the protesters met, so they could monitor the leaders' plans on their police radios. One night, Abernathy's fingers felt a small microphone on the pulpit of the Sixteenth Street Baptist Church as

Police dogs tore at marchers' clothes.

he stood to address a crowd. The police had attempted to bug the meeting. They were probably listening to his words in a patrol car nearby. For a few moments, Abernathy gave a lively speech directly to the microphone, or "doohickey."

"I want you to know, Mr. Doohickey, that we will be marching tomorrow by the hundreds. We're going to fill the jailhouses, Mr. Doohickey. We won't let anybody turn us around. We won't let the Ku Klux Klan turn us around," he said. "What's more, Mr. Doohickey, we won't let Bull Connor turn us around!"

The audience exploded in applause and laughter,

but Abernathy's message was a serious one. A march was going to take place, in spite of the injunction. It was scheduled for Good Friday, a solemn and sacred day for Christians.

Ignoring the injunction meant going to jail. And confined in a cell, Abernathy would miss the Easter service at his church. King urged him to return to Atlanta. At that moment, though, the problems in Birmingham seemed more important. Abernathy insisted that if King were going to march, then he would march and risk jailing, too.

On Good Friday, 1963, dressed in blue jeans and denim work shirts, Abernathy and King headed on foot toward the downtown shopping area. They led "a genuine army of nonviolent soldiers," Abernathy observed in his autobiography. It was a hopeful and courageous army, one that was already proclaiming victory. "Freedom has come to Birmingham!" people chanted as they walked.

Half a mile into the march, the police moved in. They arrested Abernathy, King, and 50 others. They tossed the two leaders into a dark, windowless van and hurried them off to jail.

The ministers expected to share a cell, but they were kept apart, in solitary confinement. Abernathy passed the long hours praying and reading his Bible, accepting the fact that he would be away from his family and church on Easter.

It was an unusual Easter for the Abernathy family in another way as well. Honoring the boycott, they had not purchased Easter clothes. Juanita and the children dressed in dungarees that Sunday, instead of Easter finery.

Ralph Abernathy made this a family tradition on Easter Sundays to come, long after Southern department stores were integrated. He wished to protest the commercial aspects of this religious day, his daughter Donzaleigh explained. The children learned, Donzaleigh said in a 1993 interview, that "Easter was not about going to the stores and spending money."

King used his time in jail to write an essay, "Letter from a Birmingham Jail." Writing on scraps of paper that had to be smuggled out of the building, King outlined the reasons for the Birmingham protests. The marchers were "nonviolent gadflies," King wrote, whose goal was "to create the kind of tension in society that will help men rise from the dark depths of prejudice and racism to the majestic heights of understanding and brotherhood." Several national publications printed King's words, spreading his message to all America.

The marches continued while Abernathy and

King were behind bars, but people's enthusiasm declined. Many adults feared going to jail and losing their jobs. After the two leaders were released from jail on April 20, the Southern Christian Leadership Conference urged the teenagers and children of Birmingham to join the march. The children had no jobs to lose, the march leaders reasoned.

More than 900 black young people were arrested on May 2, following a civil rights march. Some were only six years old. The next day, a thousand girls and boys stayed home from school. They gathered at the Sixteenth Street Church, ready to march. This time, Bull Connor surprised the demonstrators with a new tactic: fire hoses.

Water traveled through these hoses with great force—enough to reach flames on the upper stories of buildings. Used on human beings, the hoses became powerful weapons. The water knocked young people to the ground, pushed them against walls and curbs, and lifted them over the tops of parked cars. Some boys and girls hid behind trees to protect themselves from the watery blast. Others danced in defiance. A. G. Gaston, owner of the Gaston Motel, looked out his window to see a girl rolling helplessly down the street, carried along by the force of the water.

Hundreds of young people joined in the march.

Such cruel treatment of the children aroused great anger in their parents. More and more of them joined the protests. Abernathy urged them to continue marching and carrying signs, and never to give up. In recordings of his speeches, he can be heard telling them, "Keep moving, Birmingham!"

By Tuesday, May 7, 2,000 people were in jail. Still, the marches continued. People staged sit-ins at lunch counters and picketed stores. "Freedom! Freedom!" they shouted. "We're marching for freedom!" The police brought out the dogs and hoses once more. This time, the fast-moving water injured Fred Shuttlesworth. On hearing that a protest leader had been hurt, Bull Connor commented, "I'm sorry I missed it. I wish they'd carried him away in a hearse." Publications across the country printed his chilling words.

The tension in Birmingham reached such a high level that George Wallace, governor of Alabama, sent 500 state troopers to the city to prevent further clashes. But tension had been the goal of the "nonviolent gadflies." The downtown merchants were now ready to negotiate. Following a day of truce, on which no marches took place, the merchants agreed to end segregated fitting rooms, rest rooms, drinking fountains, and lunch counters. They promised to hire some African American salespeople.

Abernathy celebrated the victory with the other civil rights leaders, and went home to Atlanta on May 11. Shortly after he and King left town, the whites of Birmingham expressed their displeasure over the agreement. Bull Connor urged the white population to stage a boycott of their own.

The Ku Klux Klan held a rally in a Birmingham suburb. "Martin Luther King's, in our opinion, epitaph can be written here in Birmingham," threatened Robert Shelton, grand dragon of the Ku Klux Klan, on television. Most ominously of all, two bombs exploded—one at the home of A. D. King, and one at the Gaston Motel. If Ralph Abernathy and Martin Luther King had remained in the city, they might have been killed.

When a crowd of African Americans gathered at the motel to protest the explosion, the police began to strike at people with clubs. It saddened Abernathy to learn that a riot had taken place, with both blacks and whites engaging in violence.

The events in Alabama made the injustice of segregation plain to many Americans, including President John F. Kennedy. Kennedy saw that the nation faced a crisis. He asked Congress to enact a new civil rights law. This law would protect the right of all people to be served in restaurants, department stores, hotels, and any other establishments that were open to the public. It would also cut off federal funds to states and institutions that failed to comply.

"This seems to me to be an elementary right," Kennedy said in a televised speech. "Its denial is an arbitrary indignity that no American in 1963 should have to endure."

President Kennedy's civil rights act promised greater fairness and possibilities. African

Americans felt hope in the summer of 1963. Then, just one day after Kennedy told the nation about the proposed law, angry whites shot and killed Medgar Evers, a black civil rights worker, outside his Mississippi home. The hopefulness turned to despair.

Chapter / Seven

/*Jericho*

The March on Washington would soon give people back their hope.

The idea for a massive rally in the nation's capital originated with A. Philip Randolph, founder of the Brotherhood of Sleeping Car Porters, the first labor union made up mostly of black workers. Randolph wanted to call attention to the employment problems of African Americans. The unemployment rate for black workers was 114 percent higher than it was for whites in 1963. Working blacks tended to earn much less than white workers. The average white family earned $6,500 a year in 1963, while the average black family scraped by on yearly earnings of $3,500.

Randolph asked the Southern Christian Leadership Conference and other civil rights organizations to take part in the march. The civil rights leaders saw the planned gathering as a way to show public support for racial equality. The sight of thousands of people peacefully moving along the wide streets of Washington, D.C., could persuade Congress to pass the civil rights act.

The March on Washington for Jobs and Freedom was scheduled for August 28, 1963. Ralph Abernathy was on the grounds of the Washington Monument early in the morning on that day, as marchers started to arrive. By 7:00 A.M., 1,000 people had congregated. By 9:30 A.M., the number had grown to 40,000. Abernathy and the other planners hoped to see 100,000 people show up. They reached that goal by 11:00 A.M.

In all, more than 200,000 people took part in the March on Washington. They were black and white, and they came from nearly every state. They poured off trains at Washington's Union Station. Their buses crowded the roads entering the capital.

The march had been billed as a nonviolent gathering. But with so many people assembled,

Demonstrators taking part in the March on Washington proceed down Constitution Avenue.

there was always a chance that violence could break out. Abernathy and King worried that violence in Washington could undo the recent gains in the civil rights movement.

They need not have feared. August 28 was a day of peace and celebration. The crowd moved in a slow and orderly manner from the Washington Monument to the grounds of the Lincoln Memorial. "Pass that bill!" people chanted. Many carried signs: "We march for jobs for all, a decent pay NOW!" "We demands equal rights NOW!"

People filled every inch of space between the Lincoln Memorial and the Washington Monument. Some stood, craning their necks to see over the crowd. Others sat beneath trees to eat picnic lunches, or dangled their hot, tired feet in the long, shallow Reflecting Pool between the two monuments.

Singers entertained the crowd, expressing the longings and concerns of all who listened. "I'm gonna tell my Lord when I get home, just how long you've been treating me wrong," sang the famed gospel singer Mahalia Jackson.

Speakers stood before the great statue of Abraham Lincoln to call for change in American government and society. Television cameras carried their images to the nation and Europe. "This civil rights revolution is not confined to the Negroes," said A. Philip Randolph in the first speech of the day, "nor is it confined to civil rights. Our white allies cannot be free while we are not."

John Lewis, national chairman of the Student Nonviolent Coordinating Committee, a civil rights group formed by college students, called for honest and committed politicians in his speech. "What political leader," he asked, "can stand up and say, 'My party is the party of principles'?"

Lewis wanted to know, "Where is the political party that will make it unnecessary to march in the streets of Birmingham?"

Martin Luther King spoke last. The events in Montgomery and Birmingham had made King a well-known figure. People were eager to hear what he had to say.

"I have a dream," King said. He shared his dream for America's future. It was a dream that embraced all Americans, black and white, "sons of former slaves and the sons of former slave owners." It was a dream that in places such as Mississippi, "a state sweltering with the heat of injustice," people might find "an oasis of freedom and justice." It was a dream of human beings judged according to their character, and not their race.

With faith in this dream, King continued, "We shall be able to transform the jangling discords of our nation into a beautiful symphony of brotherhood."

Standing behind his friend on that hot afternoon, Ralph Abernathy was one of the millions of people moved by King's words. Abernathy reached out to embrace King as he stepped away from the podium. The speech was so powerful, Abernathy insisted that the Holy Spirit had possessed King and guided his words.

When the music and speeches ended, people dispersed, heading toward their trains and buses. For Ralph Abernathy, though, the day was not quite over. "I went back to the grounds about six or seven o'clock that evening," he said in the "Eyes on the Prize" interviews. "There was nothing but wind blowing across the reflection pool, moving and blowing and keeping music. We were so proud that no violence had taken place that day. We were so pleased. This beautiful scene of the wind dancing on the sands of the Lincoln Memorial I will never forget. This was the greatest day of my life."

The March on Washington allowed many people to come together and show their commitment and strength.

Kennedy's civil rights act became law in 1964, but African Americans continued to struggle in their daily lives. Unemployment and low wages remained problems for black men and women. And racism flourished.

On September 15, 1963, a shocking event reminded Americans that the society King had envisioned at the Lincoln Memorial was still only a dream. A bomb exploded in the Sixteenth Street Baptist Church in Birmingham, killing four teenage girls.

Young blacks who witnessed the brutality of white racists grew impatient with the slow pace of social change. Leaders such as Malcolm X, the Black Muslim minister, urged African Americans to separate themselves from white society, which he viewed as corrupt.

Increasingly, people who felt trapped by poverty and racism turned to violence themselves. During the "long, hot summer of 1964," riots erupted in the black neighborhoods of many American cities.

Abernathy and King never doubted the rightness of their nonviolent approach, although at times racial violence caused King to fear for his life. One day in early 1965, when they were riding in a car, King asked his friend to take over as head of the Southern Christian Leadership Conference if something happened to him.

Ralph Abernathy never strove to be a famous man. He had always worked selflessly for civil rights, caring more about the goals of the movement than any personal recognition. He hated to think about the possibility of King's death. He had trouble imagining himself taking on King's leadership role, without a best friend's counsel and advice. The two were a team. Reluctantly, he agreed to King's request.

King and Abernathy held that conversation as they traveled toward Selma, a city in Dallas County, Alabama, to work for voting rights. Blacks were still blocked from registering to vote in the South, just as they were when Abernathy was in college. Only one-fifth of Alabama's eligible blacks were registered to vote in 1964. Things were even worse in Mississippi, where only 7 percent of African Americans over age 21 were on the voting rolls.

More than half of the 29,000 people who lived in Selma were black, yet blacks made up only 3 percent of Selma's registered voters. The Student Nonviolent Coordinating Committee had been trying to register black voters in Selma for three years, with little success. Repeatedly, Sheriff Jim Clark and his deputies blocked their efforts. The whites in power were determined to keep tight control over the city's politics and economy. At last, Amelia Boynton, a member of a Selma voting rights group, turned to the Southern Christian Leadership Conference.

Abernathy's work in Selma began with daily marches from Brown Chapel, a local church, to the Dallas County Court House, the place for voter registration. On January 18, 1965, Sheriff Clark met the first group of marchers at the courthouse door. He told them to wait in a nearby alley. They would be called in to register one at a time. The group obeyed, although they were sure Clark was lying. No one, they knew, would register to vote that day. "We had waited almost two hundred years and we could wait a little bit longer," Abernathy wrote in his memoirs.

The next day, the marchers refused to wait in the alley. Clark grabbed Amelia Boynton by the collar of her coat and shoved her toward a police car. The other marchers called to her, "Go on, Mrs. Boynton, you don't have to be in jail by yourself." They reassured her that they would soon be there, too. In fact, more than 50 people went to jail that day.

Speaking that night at Brown Chapel, Abernathy thanked Jim Clark for arresting those people and attracting attention to their cause. He proposed making Clark an honorary member of the Southern Christian Leadership Conference!

The marches continued, and the number of arrests grew. Abernathy thought of the biblical hero Joshua. Following Moses' death, Joshua led the Hebrews across the Jordan River and into the promised land. Joshua also destroyed the corrupt city of Jericho. For days, he and his army marched around Jericho's thick walls. The people of Jericho watched them, wondering when Joshua would attack. The assault never came, however. It was God, said the Bible, who caused the walls of Jericho to tumble down.

The civil rights marchers' persistence would be rewarded, Abernathy believed, when Selma's barriers of racism tumbled down as well. "We were marching around the walls of Jericho and the white establishment knew it," he wrote in his autobiography.

A federal judge at last barred county officials from blocking voter registration. When African Americans again tried to register, however, the county workers dragged their heels, processing only a few new voters each day.

Abernathy, King, and their colleagues were far from satisfied. They held a mass march and got themselves arrested. They hoped to draw the eyes of the nation to Selma, through the news media.

Whenever they shared a jail cell, King and Abernathy followed the same routine. They fasted for two days. They prayed, meditated, and sang hymns. Gandhi had followed a similar regimen whenever he was imprisoned. This time, the jailers placed Abernathy and King in a large cell with all of the men who had been arrested. All of the prisoners—both marchers and convicted criminals—cheered to see the two leaders walk through the heavy prison doors.

Abernathy read to the men from the small Bible he carried in his pocket. He chose words from the Twenty-seventh Psalm to give them courage.

> *The Lord is my light and my salvation;*
>   *whom shall I fear?*
> *The Lord is the strength of my life;*
>   *of whom shall I be afraid?*

Malcolm X traveled to Selma while Abernathy and King were in jail. He spoke to the city's African Americans at Brown Chapel. "The white people should thank Dr. King for holding people in check, for there are others who do not believe in these measures," he said. He advised the black residents of Selma to present their grievances to the president at the White House and to the world community at the United Nations.

Juanita Abernathy and Coretta Scott King, fearing people would be aroused to violence, calmed the crowd in their husbands' place. They reminded the audience of the importance of peaceful protest.

The resolve to remain nonviolent faced a

difficult test on February 18, when the African Americans of nearby Marion, Alabama, held a nighttime march. Without warning, the street lights went out. The police set upon the marchers in the darkness, beating them with nightsticks. They hit 26-year-old Jimmie Lee Jackson in the face with a stick and shot him in the abdomen. Jackson died a week later.

It rained in Selma on the day of Jimmie Jackson's funeral. A white banner that hung above the doors of Brown Chapel proclaimed, "Racism killed our brother."

The Reverend Ralph Abernathy, released from jail, spoke to the mourners at Jackson's grave site. He acknowledged the young man's place in American history. "Jimmie Jackson has joined the ranks of the many martyrs who have fallen along the way in building this great nation and bringing us to this hour," he said. Abernathy cautioned that before the marches ended, "You and I might take our rightful place beside him."

"We must not be bitter and we must not harbor ideas of retaliating with violence," King reminded the grieving black population.

Privately, Abernathy and King feared that the people's anger might erupt into violence. They searched for a way to channel people's emotions into positive action. They announced that a great 50-mile march would take place, from Selma to Montgomery, the state capital. The marchers would deliver a list of their demands to Governor George Wallace.

"Such a march cannot and will not be tolerated," Wallace said in a public statement. He issued an order forbidding the demonstration.

The Selma-to-Montgomery march was scheduled to start on Sunday, March 7, despite the governor's order. Abernathy and King had to be in Atlanta to conduct church services on that day, so Hosea Williams of the Southern Christian Leadership Conference led the march, along with John Lewis of the Student Nonviolent Coordinating Committee.

Williams and Lewis led 500 marchers over the Edmund Pettus Bridge, which carried them out of Selma and onto the highway. That was as far as they went. State troopers and county police officers, on foot and on horseback, were waiting for them. The police ordered the marchers to return to Brown Chapel. Then, before the marchers could comply, Major John Cloud of the state police called out, "Troopers forward!"

The police attacked the unarmed demonstrators with whips, chains, rubber tubing, and electric

Marchers are stopped by police after crossing the Edmund Pettus Bridge.

cattle prods. Choking clouds of tear gas filled the air as people scrambled out of the path of the horses' hooves and back across the bridge.

Abernathy listened to news reports of the violence on his car radio in the parking lot of his church. On that day, called Bloody Sunday, more than 100 people received injuries in the violence in Selma. Fifty African Americans needed treatment at a hospital.

Wasting no time, Abernathy and King flew to Selma. They planned to lead a new march to Montgomery on March 9, but first they went to federal court to seek an order keeping Wallace and his state troopers away. Instead, however, the judge surprised them. He ordered the protesters not to march. He wanted some time to think the matter over.

Abernathy and King hated to defy a federal court order. Yet they did not want to abandon their work in Selma. They decided to hold a symbolic march.

On the planned day, 1,500 people, black and white, followed King and Abernathy out of Brown Chapel. Singing, "Ain't gonna let nobody turn me 'round," they crossed the bridge and stood 50 feet away from the waiting troopers. They had reached the site of the Bloody Sunday attack. Abernathy turned to face the mass of people and asked them to kneel. He then led them in a prayer that summed up the events in Selma and his people's concerns for the future. The crowd turned around and walked peacefully back to Brown Chapel.

And then the Selma campaign claimed its second life. Outraged whites attacked the Reverend James Reeb, a white minister from Boston who had come to Selma to march. Reeb died of a head injury. This new violence caused a public outcry. Americans called upon their leaders in Washington to pass a voting rights law. President Lyndon Johnson spoke to the nation on television. "It is not just Negroes, but all of us, who must overcome the legacy of bigotry and injustice," he said.

Johnson asked the federal court to issue an

order allowing the Selma-to-Montgomery march. He telephoned Governor Wallace and told him to keep the police away from the protesters. He ordered the National Guard to protect the people who marched.

The Alabama Freedom March began on Sunday, March 21. Outside Brown Chapel, King spoke with great feeling to the people who had gathered. "Those of us who are Negroes don't have much. We have known the long night of poverty," he said. "Because of the system, we don't have much education and some of us don't know how to make our nouns and verbs agree. But thank God we have our bodies, our feet, and our souls."

Abernathy stepped forward when King finished speaking, as he so often did, to stir up the people's enthusiasm. "Wallace, it's all over now," he called out.

More than 3,000 people set out on Highway 80. "Oh, Wallace! Segregation's got to fall," they sang. "You can never jail us all." Three hundred of them would walk the entire 50 miles. They ate meals supplied by black families who lived along the route. They slept in large tents or in cars.

Four days later, on March 25, 30,000 people joined them to march the last few miles into

Abernathy catches up on the latest news as he and Martin Luther King, Jr., lead civil rights marchers on the second day of the Selma to Montgomery march.

Montgomery. Abernathy warmly greeted Juanita and their three children, who had come to be with him. The children led the marchers up one of Montgomery's streets.

Later that day, Abernathy introduced Martin Luther King to an enormous crowd as Governor George Wallace peeked through the blinds on his office window. "As God called Joshua to lead His people across the Jordan," said Abernathy, "so also He called Martin Luther King to go to Montgomery and tell Pharaoh Wallace, 'Let my people go.'"

King's words were a statement of triumph. "They told us we wouldn't get here, and there were those who said we would get here only over their dead bodies, but all the world today knows that we are here and that we are standing before the forces of power in the state of Alabama saying, 'We ain't goin' to let nobody turn us around.'"

Thanks to the effort of thousands of people in Selma and other Southern communities, Congress passed a voting rights bill in the summer of 1965. The new law authorized federal examiners to register eligible voters. It also ended such discriminatory practices as literacy tests. The number of blacks registered to vote in the South tripled over the next four years.

The victory in Selma cost the lives of Jimmie Lee Jackson, the Reverend James Reeb, and Viola Liuzzo, a white woman from Detroit. Liuzzo, the mother of five children, had come to lend a hand during the Alabama Freedom March. She was driving some marchers back to Selma on the night of March 25 when a car carrying Ku Klux Klan members pulled up beside her. Someone in that car aimed a rifle at Liuzzo and shot her in the head.

Ralph Abernathy enjoyed spending time with his family

Chapter /Eight

/*This Lonesome Valley*

Civil rights marches, rallies, and jailings often kept Ralph Abernathy away from home for long stretches. This was hard for a man like Abernathy, who loved family life. He made sure that the time he spent with Juanita and the children was happy and memorable.

In 1993, Donzaleigh Abernathy and Ralph Abernathy III spoke about the time they spent with their father, especially the Sundays. "He would always be in a great, new, vibrant spirit on Sunday morning," recalled Ralph Abernathy III. "On Sunday mornings, he always found a joy that would be a different joy from that which he had throughout the whole week."

"He would like to make a big breakfast, regardless of his schedule," Donzaleigh Abernathy added. The reverend set the breakfast table himself. Soon, he had bacon and pancakes frying and grits bubbling in a pot. His son Ralph remembered him calling out to the family, "Wake up, wake up! It's time to get up to serve the Lord. Thank God for being alive. Thank God for this beautiful day!"

"We would always look forward to that, and be laughing and kidding around," said Ralph Abernathy III. "Quite honestly, when I got a little older it used to frustrate me, because I would have stayed out late Saturday night and would not want my father to wake me up!"

Sometimes when his children think about Abernathy, a certain Christmas comes to mind. The civil rights leader had spent the day before the holiday in jail and was unable to buy presents for the children. Donzaleigh said that he told her, "We'll just get what we need after Christmas."

Instead of playing with new toys, the children spent Christmas Day thinking about the religious meaning of the holiday. They celebrated the birth of Christianity. Disappointed at first, the children learned they could enjoy Christmas without opening presents. It was a lesson well learned. Even today, the Abernathys buy few Christmas presents for one another.

Ralph Abernathy encouraged his children to pursue their goals and make the most of their abilities. He often recited catchy phrases and rhymes that summed up the wisdom he wished to pass along. His children Donzaleigh and Ralph repeated some of those sayings in 1993 interviews. "When you give up your dreams, you die a little inside," Abernathy taught the children. "You can be anything you want to be."

He said many times, "If the elevator to success is broken, take the stairs."

"If you can't be a tree, then be a bush," Abernathy liked to say. "If you can't be a bush, then be a shrub. But be the best little shrub by the side of the road."

In the early 1960s, Ralph and Juanita asked the girls if they wished to attend the Spring Street School, a private school, along with the children of Martin Luther King, Jr. (Ralph III was not yet old enough to be a pupil there.) The children would be the first blacks to attend the school, their parents warned, and they were likely to meet with hostility. Eager to do their part for civil rights, Juandalynn and Donzaleigh agreed to go.

The anger and hatred they faced were worse than they had expected. "The kids were awful. They were mean to us," said Donzaleigh. Ralph Abernathy counseled his daughters not to fight back. He urged them to be patient and use nonviolence to teach other children that racism is wrong. "They are ignorant," he said.

"I never heard him say a cruel thing about anybody. He was always finding the good," Donzaleigh noted.

As a father, Abernathy displayed his own patience again and again. He never punished the children when they misbehaved. According to Donzaleigh, he told them instead, "You have hurt me. You have hurt me terribly."

"If we did something very bad," said Donzaleigh, "he would cry."

A devoted parent, Abernathy was willing to face danger to make his children happy. One night, the family was driving on Highway 80 in Alabama, on their way to visit relatives in Linden. Juandalynn and Donzaleigh complained that they were hungry. Abernathy was determined to buy his daughters something to eat, even though blacks were unwelcome in the businesses along that strip of roadway.

Abernathy pulled into the parking lot of a

white-owned diner. Leaving his family in the car, he faced insults and the threat of physical harm to buy two hamburgers and two soft drinks.

In 1966, Abernathy left his family in Atlanta and flew to Chicago, Illinois. The Reverend Jesse Jackson, a young minister working for the Southern Christian Leadership Conference, wanted Abernathy and King to see the poor conditions in which African Americans lived in that Northern city.

Jackson drove the civil rights leaders through slum neighborhoods on the South Side and West Side of the city, where most of Chicago's blacks lived. Abernathy saw mile after mile of crumbling houses. Because their landlords never bothered to make repairs, the residents of these neighborhoods put up with leaking roofs and broken plumbing. The many trash heaps and broken windows that he saw reminded Abernathy of the bombed-out buildings in Europe at the end of World War II.

Throughout the 20th century, many African Americans had left small towns in the South to start new lives in Northern cities. Hundreds of thousands came to Chicago, looking for jobs in factories or in the city's meatpacking industry. Chicago's black population went from 44,000 in 1910 to 234,000 in 1930. During the 1940s, the

Abernathy toured the run-down neighborhoods of Chicago where most of the city's blacks lived.

number of blacks in Chicago grew to 492,000. The total reached one million in the 1960s, and African Americans continued to arrive—even though the promise of jobs no longer existed.

No laws enforced segregation in Chicago, but white residents found ways to keep blacks from settling in their neighborhoods. White real estate agents refused to show houses in white communities to their black customers. Banks turned down mortgage applications from black men and women. Whites even employed violence to keep their neighborhoods segregated. For example, when a black couple bought a house in the all-white suburb of Cicero, Illinois, in 1951, a mob shouted insults at them, broke their windows, and damaged the outside of their home.

Chicago's white mayor in 1966, Richard Daley, controlled many aspects of city life. He dominated the police force and the labor unions. Abernathy compared Daley to the biblical king Herod, a clever and ruthless leader of the Israelites. Herod cared more about pleasing the rich than helping his subjects. According to the Bible, Herod had many babies and young children put to death when he learned the Messiah, or Savior, had been born. He feared the child would grow up to steal his power. Jesus escaped the fate of the other infants when his parents took him to Egypt.

Abernathy suspected that Mayor Daley, like Herod, might take drastic steps to hold on to his power and keep Chicago segregated.

Yet when the Southern Christian Leadership Conference began to lead marches in Chicago, Daley seemed ready to help. He promised housing repairs and integrated schools. But as Abernathy and King soon learned, Daley liked to make promises—and then do nothing. Weeks went by, and the city government failed to act.

Also, Daley's police force did nothing to help the marchers when angry whites threw rocks and bottles at them. The flying objects hit Jesse Jackson and other demonstrators. "In Chicago we sometimes had the feeling that this huge sea of snarling white faces was going to sweep over us and kill every single black marcher," Abernathy later wrote in his autobiography.

At one demonstration, white spectators turned over 15 cars belonging to African Americans. The violence was worsening. Fearing that blacks might fight back, Daley agreed to sit down with King, Abernathy, and the other black leaders and work out a plan to end the unfair housing practices by law. Daley gave the Southern Christian Leadership Conference his guarantee that the city would make improvements to its black neighborhoods. Abernathy and King remained wary, but they let the mayor have another chance to help his city's blacks.

"This is a great day for Chicago," Daley announced to the press when the meetings ended. Again, however, he forgot the promises he had made. It would be years before Chicago had an open housing ordinance, a law that protected African Americans from discrimination when buying or renting homes.

Today, many African Americans reside in the suburbs of Chicago, places that were once all white. But many more remain in the inner city, trapped by poverty and racism. Chicago, like most

American cities, has much work to do to solve its racial and economic problems.

When he had time to look back, Abernathy saw the Chicago campaign as a failure of the civil rights movement. But he preferred to look toward the future. New projects kept beckoning. There was still so much injustice in America. There was still so much that needed to be done.

In the 1960s, Abernathy and King came to understand the true extent of poverty in the United States. They visited a school in Marks, Mississippi. The thin, impoverished children who attended the school had nothing for lunch but a few crackers and a slice of an apple. "And when Dr. King saw that, and that is all they had for lunch, he actually ended up crying," Abernathy said in an interview for television. "The tears came streaming down his cheek. And he had to leave the room."

For weeks after they left Marks, the two men were haunted by the memory of those small boys and girls. Every school day, those children struggled to learn. Every day of their lives, they had too little to eat. And they were just a few of the 20 million Americans who lived below the poverty level. The poor often felt invisible, living in ghettos and small towns, away from middle-class communities.

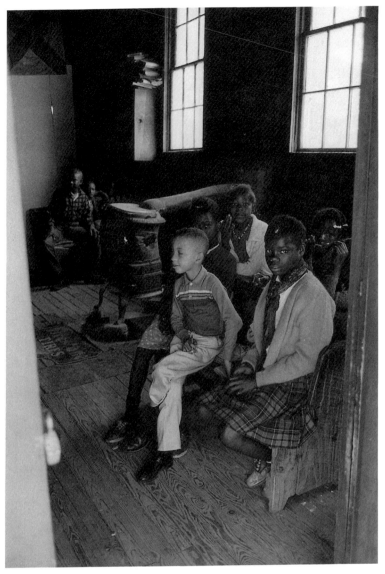

Even after the Supreme Court outlawed school segregation in 1954, impoverished black children in the South attended schools far inferior to those in middle-class communities.

Poverty weighed heavily on people in inner-city neighborhoods. For three hot summers in the late 1960s, that pressure led to violence. Sixty-seven riots occurred in cities across the United States. Eighty people died. More and more, younger black leaders favored violence as a method for change. They urged African Americans to fight for their rights. "The rebellions that we see are merely dress rehearsals for the revolution that is to come," warned H. Rap Brown of the Student Nonviolent Coordinating Committee.

Abernathy and King resolved to do something about the problem of poverty. They decided to hold a Poor People's Campaign. They planned to bring the poor to Washington, D.C., to let the government and the American people see first-hand the poverty that existed in their prosperous nation.

King saw this campaign as "an alternative to riots." As he explained at a press conference, "This is a kind of last, desperate demand for the nation to respond to nonviolence."

Some legislators had shown concern for the needs of the poor, and this gave the civil rights leaders hope. Senator Robert Kennedy of New York had come to Mississippi to see firsthand the way poor Southern blacks lived. As he toured the farms and shacks, Kennedy asked a young boy what he had eaten for lunch. "I didn't have lunch yet," the boy answered.

Kennedy patted the boy's cheek. The senator's face showed that he understood what the child felt ashamed to say. He would have nothing for lunch that day.

In the spring of 1968, Abernathy and King took time out from planning the Poor People's Campaign. They went to Memphis, Tennessee, to help striking garbage collectors. These workers, nearly all of whom were black, had several grievances against the city of Memphis. First, they were tired of working for low pay. One worker explained that he could not support his seven children on wages of $1.04 per hour. Second, the men were angered after two black sanitation workers were killed on the job and their families received no compensation. Finally, the workers resented the city's refusal to recognize their labor union.

When the striking workers marched in protest, an army of police officers herded them to the side of the street. The police assaulted the protesters with nightsticks and Mace, a chemical that causes tears, dizziness, and nausea. "Nobody was safe in Memphis," the Reverend James Smith, a local minister, told journalists. The African Americans of Memphis asked the Southern Christian Leadership Conference to come to their city to help them.

To Abernathy and King, the strike in Memphis was linked to the Poor People's Campaign. America needed to know that some of its workers labored for mere starvation wages.

The two civil rights leaders arrived in Memphis on March 28 to conduct a peaceful demonstration. However, a group called the Invaders—young blacks who favored violent protest—were among the thousands who walked with Abernathy and King. Soon, Abernathy heard shouts and the sound of breaking windows. The Invaders were turning the march into a riot.

Fearing that their lives and their entire nonviolent movement were in danger, the two ministers decided to leave the site of the trouble. Bernard Lee, King's assistant, flagged down a passing car. The woman behind the wheel agreed to let Abernathy and King ride in her car to safety.

Ralph Abernathy and Martin Luther King stayed in a Memphis hotel room while the protesters and police battled in the streets. Sixty people would be injured that day, and a 16-year-old boy would die. Many stores would be damaged. Sad and exhausted, King fell asleep. Abernathy covered his friend with a bedspread. He had never known King to be this depressed.

Abernathy and King left Memphis on Friday, March 29, promising to return. That night, back in Atlanta, Coretta and Martin Luther King ate dinner at the home of Ralph and Juanita Abernathy. It was the last time the four old friends would spend an evening together.

On April 3, Abernathy and King returned to Memphis to organize another march. They hoped it would be a peaceful one.

King was scheduled to speak at Memphis's Masonic Temple that night, but his heart was not in it. He was still tired, and the weather was very bad. "It was raining, raining, and wind was blowing everywhere," Abernathy explained in the "Eyes on the Prize" series. "I believe a little tornado came to Memphis also. And he knew that there would not be a big crowd." King asked Abernathy and Jesse Jackson to speak in his place.

Abernathy arrived at the Masonic Temple to see news reporters and photographers standing in the rain. Inside, 300 people sat in an auditorium that could hold 3,000. Abernathy understood that those people had braved the terrible weather to listen to Martin Luther King. He hated to disappoint them. Abernathy telephoned his friend at the Lorraine Motel, where the staff of the Southern Christian Leadership Conference was staying, to say that the audience wanted to hear King. King replied that he would be there.

Fifteen minutes later, Abernathy introduced Martin Luther King to the audience. King stepped up to the podium and said, "I want everybody here to know that Ralph David Abernathy is the closest and dearest friend I have in the world!"

That night, King made his famous speech about viewing the promised land. He spoke like a man approaching the end of his life. Later, many men and women would say that his words seemed to foretell the future.

"I don't know what will happen now. We've got some difficult days ahead. But it really doesn't matter to me now, because I've been to the mountaintop," King said. He finished his remarks by telling the crowd, "I'm happy tonight. I'm not worried about anything. I'm not fearing any man. Mine eyes have seen the glory of the coming of the Lord."

When the speech ended, Abernathy stepped forward to embrace his friend. For the rest of his life, he would remember that evening. He would treasure the first words of King's speech: "Ralph David Abernathy is the closest and dearest friend I have in the world."

The next evening, Abernathy, King, and

others from the Southern Christian Leadership Conference had been invited to dinner at the home of a Memphis minister. As he splashed on cologne inside the motel room, getting ready to go, Abernathy could hear King on the balcony outside. King was talking to Jesse Jackson, who stood in the courtyard of the motel. They talked about the meal they expected to enjoy. The minister's wife was cooking some of King's favorite foods—roast beef, chitterlings, candied yams, and corn bread.

Then Abernathy heard a sharp crack that sounded like an exploding firecracker. He looked through the open door of the motel room to the balcony where King had been standing. Abernathy recounted the events that followed for the authors of several books and articles. He spoke about the occurrences of April 4, 1968, with Dick Gregory, co-author of the book *Murder in Memphis.*

"All I could see was his feet," Abernathy said to Gregory. Abernathy rushed out to the balcony to see King lying, fallen and bleeding, on the concrete floor. The crack Abernathy had heard was the sound of a gun. Martin Luther King had been shot.

Abernathy bent down and held the wounded

man in his arms. He assured King that everything would be all right. According to Dick Gregory, Abernathy told King, "I'll get help, don't worry."

Everyone who heard the shot rushed toward the balcony. Andrew Young, executive vice president of the Southern Christian Leadership Conference, saw the seriousness of King's wounds. He told Abernathy that for King, "It's over." But Abernathy was unwilling to face that fact.

A devoted friend, as ever, Abernathy rode along in the ambulance that took King to a Memphis hospital. He stayed in the operating room while a team of doctors desperately tried to save King's life. A little while later, one of the doctors told Abernathy that King would not survive. Andrew Young had been correct. For Martin Luther King, Jr., it was over.

King died that evening in the arms of Ralph David Abernathy. In the hours that followed, Abernathy performed the sad but necessary tasks that accompanied King's death. He made a formal identification of the body at the city morgue. "I remember something that hurt me more than anything else that night," he said to Dick Gregory. "I remember going to that morgue and seeing my good friend with a brown paper tag hooked to his toe. I'll never forget that sight." Abernathy also gave permission for the coroner to perform an autopsy—an operation to determine the exact cause of death—on King's body.

That night, the nation learned that Martin Luther King had been assassinated. Many people were so upset by the news that they lost control of their emotions and their actions. Riots occurred in the African American sections of Chicago, Washington, D.C., and other cities. Dozens of people died.

Police officers in Memphis arrested a white man with a criminal record, James Earl Ray, and charged him with the murder of Martin Luther King, Jr.

Ralph Abernathy struggled privately with his grief. "I felt that I had lost part of me," he said in an interview for television. "I felt that I had to walk this lonesome valley now by myself."

The people of the Southern Christian Leadership Conference pledged to continue their work together. Abernathy listened as staff member James Bevel told the rest of the group that he had loved Dr. King. But with King dead, he urged the others to rally behind their new leader, Ralph David Abernathy.

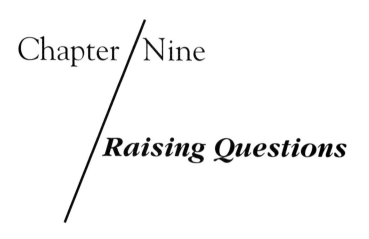

Chapter / Nine

Raising Questions

On Sunday morning, April 7, the Reverend Ralph David Abernathy faced his congregation at the West Hunter Street Baptist Church. Instead of preaching a sermon that morning, he read a letter. It was his last letter to Martin Luther King, Jr., written after King's death. It was a letter his friend would never see. As he read, Abernathy gave voice to the thoughts that had filled his mind since King's death.

Abernathy imagined King in Heaven, meeting the prophets of the Bible and people who had died before. In his letter, he asked King to visit the people who had died for the cause of civil rights, people such as Jimmie Lee Jackson, Viola Liuzzo, and the four girls killed in the bombing of the Sixteenth Street Baptist Church.

Abernathy asked King to look up Malcolm X, who had been shot to death in New York City just weeks after going to Selma. "Malcolm may not have believed what we believe," said Abernathy, "but he was a child of God and he was concerned about the welfare of his people."

Next, Abernathy turned to the past. He recalled the first time he saw King and heard him preach in Atlanta. Following custom, everyone present had shaken hands with King when the church service ended. Abernathy could still recall the feel of that handshake. "It was warm and strong. It was soft and tender. I liked you even then," he wrote to his friend.

The letter traced the route the two ministers took through the South, working for their people: from Montgomery to Birmingham to Washington, D.C., and, finally, to Memphis and King's death. "You who had been our spokesman couldn't speak anymore," Abernathy said. He was certain, though, that King's words "will live in our minds and our hearts and in the souls of black men and white men, brown men and yellow men as long as time shall last."

Abernathy assured King that the quest for equality would continue. "Don't worry, my friend. We will pull our load. We will do our best," he said.

As Abernathy spoke in his church, mourners filed past King's casket in Sisters Chapel at Atlanta's Spelman College. They would do so for hours.

The next day, Abernathy returned to Memphis to lead the peaceful march for the striking garbage workers. It was the march King had been planning on the day he died. Abernathy and the others walked in silence as they honored the memory of Martin Luther King. The Memphis city government would later meet with the sanitation workers and agree to their demands.

And then on Tuesday, April 9, Martin Luther King, Jr., was laid to rest. Millions of Americans watched the funeral on television. They saw the Reverend Ralph Abernathy, dressed in his pastor's robes, at the site of King's grave. Abernathy sprinkled white flower petals on King's casket. He recited words that had been repeated in countless graveside rituals: "Ashes to ashes, dust to dust."

Martin Luther King now belonged to history, but for Ralph Abernathy, life went on. He began the most challenging period of his life, his years as president of the Southern Christian Leadership Conference. In the months preceding his death,

Abernathy visits the grave of slain civil rights leader Martin Luther King, Jr.

King had committed himself to helping America's poor. Abernathy vowed to carry out the plans he and King had made together.

The Poor People's Campaign would be the most ambitious project Abernathy had ever undertaken. He planned to bring thousands of impoverished Americans, from every part of the country, to Washington, D.C. They would create a settlement in the center of the city, among the gleaming monuments and government buildings. It would be a place where the poor could live.

In Memphis, Abernathy spoke to the first group of protesters heading for Washington. "For any of you who would linger in the cemetery and tarry around the grave, I have news for you. We have business on the road to freedom," he told his followers. "We must prove to white America that you can kill the dreamer, but you cannot kill the dream."

Abernathy knew there were no easy solutions to the problems that faced the poor. "The press asks me, 'Well, what bills do you want written in Washington?'" he said to an audience of young African Americans in Jackson, Mississippi. "It's not my job to write bills. My job is to raise questions."

Abernathy raised tough questions: How can the nation ensure that every person has enough food and a decent home? Can we provide a job that pays a decent wage to every man or woman seeking work? Tackling these issues would mean changing society's values. Americans would need to value sharing and helping others rather than acquiring wealth and possessions. The government, which was spending millions to support an unpopular war in Vietnam, would need to change its values as well.

In early May, just a month after King's death, thousands of poor Americans set out for Washington, D.C. They came from Marks, Mississippi, where the sight of poor, hungry children first touched Abernathy and King, and from Selma, Alabama, site of the voting rights campaign. They came from Georgia, New Mexico, and Appalachia, from Milwaukee and New York City. Most traveled by bus. But many traveled at least part of the way in wagons pulled by mules.

Abernathy went to rural Mississippi at the start of the campaign. Two mules—the work animals of the poor—had been hitched to a wagon there, to carry people toward Washington. The protesters had named the mules Eastland and Stennis, after Mississippi's two U.S. senators.

Wearing denim clothing and heavy work shoes, Abernathy spoke with humor to the people starting their journey. Journalists had their tape recorders and cameras rolling, and many newspapers and television broadcasts would carry his speech. "That mule is named Eastland," Abernathy said. "I didn't know why. Then I found out that he's old and forgetful, and he doesn't even want to carry his part of the load. The other's Stennis. They gave me the task to lead him. Now, Stennis is still full of life. But he's so stubborn. He wanted to get off the road to eat grass. I said, 'All these years, you've been leading us around, but today, thanks be to God, we're leading you.'"

Everyone laughed. Some people remarked that before the gains of the civil rights movement, an African American would not have dared to poke fun at a white senator in the South.

Already, the press was comparing Abernathy to King. Reporters looked for flaws in his leadership and predicted failure for him. "Don't ever get it in your mind it was Martin Luther King's dream only," Abernathy told a black church audience in Selma. "It was Ralph David Abernathy's dream too. I never tried to preach like him and he never tried to preach like me." The new leader insisted he had talents and abilities of his own to offer. "I'm not going to be anybody but Ralph Abernathy," he said.

The first groups of poor people arrived in Washington, D.C., on May 18. The Southern Christian Leadership Conference had obtained a permit to occupy Potomac Park, near the Lincoln Memorial. Upon his arrival at the site, Abernathy acknowledged that the land had once belonged to the Native Americans. People listening to Abernathy in Washington or in news broadcasts at home heard him ask Linda Aranayko, a member of the Creek tribe, "Is it all right if we use this land?"

"Yes," Aranayko replied.

Abernathy then hammered a stake into the ground, starting construction of the new settlement. "I declare this to be the site of our new city, Resurrection City, U.S.A.," he said. Many people then got busy putting together plywood A-frame huts. They built 600 shelters, enough to house 3,000 people.

The huts were simple and small, but they were more comfortable than the homes many of the poor had left behind. "I'm doing much better here than I was in Mississippi," said one woman.

A man living at Resurrection City with his wife and daughter said their shanty was their first real home. "It's beautiful, man," he commented.

Resurrection City was to be a model city, a

place where people of different races lived in harmony and everyone's needs were met. It was a real city, with telephone lines, electricity, and plumbing. It even had its own Zip Code.

The residents of the new city ate together in a large tent. They chanted phrases that expressed the pride they felt in themselves.

> *I am somebody.*
> *I may be uneducated,*
> *But I am somebody.*
> *I may be unemployed,*
> *But I am somebody.*

Led by Abernathy, Jesse Jackson, and others, they marched to the offices of the Department of Labor and the Department of Agriculture to state their need for jobs and food. News reporters were often on hand. But instead of focusing on the demonstrations and the needs of the poor, the reporters wrote about anything that went wrong at Resurrection City.

They wrote stories about the mud that filled the settlement's paths and roadways. Washington had a very wet spring that year. Eight inches of rain fell in six weeks. Once, it rained for three days and two nights without stopping. Potomac

Park grew soggy and covered with puddles. Newspapers and magazines printed pictures of adults pushing cars through deep mud. They showed children floating rafts on huge puddles.

News articles also described incidents of violence. Some of the young people who came to Resurrection City belonged to gangs. They stole things, vandalized property, and harassed people on the streets. Abernathy sent most of the gang members home, but a few remained and continued to cause trouble.

Abernathy and Jackson tried to remain hopeful in spite of the press reports, but on June 6, a major news bulletin lowered the spirits of everyone at Resurrection City. Robert Kennedy had been shot and killed in California. Kennedy had been campaigning for the Democratic party's nomination for president. Throughout his political career, he had shown a commitment to equality and a concern for the poor. He had offered hope to many blacks and poor Americans.

A train carried Kennedy's body to Washington, D.C. As his funeral procession moved toward Arlington National Cemetery, across the Potomac River from the capital, it stopped at Resurrection City. A school choir sang "The Battle Hymn of the Republic" from the steps of the Lincoln Memorial. Many people at Resurrection City sang along.

On June 19, Ralph Abernathy stood on the Lincoln Memorial steps. The occasion was a rally known as Solidarity Day. Between 50,000 and 100,000 people had come together to hear speeches and show their support for programs to help the poor. "We will stay in Washington and fight nonviolently," Abernathy told the crowd, "until the nation rises up and demands real assurance that our needs will be met."

But there would be no uprising. The following weekend, the Southern Christian Leadership Conference's permit to use Potomac Park expired, and the National Park Service refused to renew it.

Abernathy planned one last march to the U.S. Capitol. On a rainy morning, he led more than 200 people toward the building that houses the Congress. When police stopped their progress, the marchers sat down to block a street and sidewalk. They were immediately arrested. While they were in jail, Park Service workers took down the plywood huts of Resurrection City. The model city existed no longer.

Ralph Abernathy left Washington with small victories. Congress had passed a housing bill. The Office of Economic Opportunity had allocated

$25 million for poverty relief. The Department of
Agriculture had arranged to extend its food stamp
program to 330 counties. And the Welfare
Department had promised to consider national
standards for state welfare programs.

Abernathy had pricked the nation's
conscience, though. After the lesson of
Resurrection City, Americans no longer could say
they did not know the extent of poverty in their
rich nation. Abernathy had succeeded in his
mission to raise questions.

And his work for the poor would go on. There
were other ways to help people improve their standard of living. There were campaigns that might
achieve definite results. The 1969 hospital workers' strike in Charleston, South Carolina, was one
such campaign.

Nearly all of the men and women who held
the lowest-paying jobs in Charleston's hospitals
were African Americans. These men and women
worked in the hospitals' laundries and kitchens.
They cleaned rooms and waxed floors. Earning
$1.30 per hour, many could barely afford to pay
their bills. Some of the hospital workers had
formed a labor union, an organization to work for
better pay and job conditions.

Then, in April, one of the hospitals fired 12

workers who were union organizers. Four hundred hospital workers responded by going on strike. The hospitals where they had worked quickly hired other people to take their place.

The hospital strike in Charleston reminded Ralph Abernathy of the sanitation workers' strike in Memphis just one year earlier. In both cases, most of the people on strike were black. The mayor of Memphis had refused to negotiate with the garbage collectors' union. Now, the Charleston city government ignored the hospital workers. A state law barred any government agency from bargaining with a union, they said.

The potential for violence existed in both cities. Martin Luther King, Jr., had lost his life while aiding the strikers in Memphis. There was a chance, Abernathy knew, that he could be assassinated, too. Abernathy assured the hospital workers that he would march for their cause, even if his actions led to his death. He spoke about the risks he faced to the congregation of his church. "If a man has not found something he's willing to die for," he said, "then he's not fit to live."

After the first demonstration outside Charleston County Hospital, a judge issued an order forbidding more than ten people from marching together at once. Abernathy defied the injunction. On April 21, he led a large group to picket the hospital. The next day, he brought more than 700 people to kneel and pray outside the building.

When he wasn't leading protest marches, Abernathy met with lawyers for the Southern Christian Leadership Conference. He wanted to challenge the state law against bargaining with unions. The lawyers told Abernathy that changing the law would be very difficult. But maybe, if the hospital workers called their organization by a name other than union, the mayor's office would meet with them.

The hospital workers liked this idea. They offered to call off their strike if the people who had been fired regained their jobs, and if an organization—not a union—could bargain on their behalf. While the government officials thought the matter over, the strikers marched again.

With Juanita at his side, Abernathy led a demonstration outside Medical College Hospital. When he crossed a line of waiting police officers, he was arrested. The protest continued while Abernathy was in jail, and the protesters became violent. Young blacks threw rocks, bottles, and even firebombs.

Abernathy's lawyers paid his bail, which is

money pledged as security to allow him to be set free. Released from jail, he pleaded for nonviolence. But the destructiveness worsened, and clashes with the police grew more frequent.

The police arrested Abernathy again, and this time they charged him with a felony, or serious crime. They charged him with inciting, or encouraging, people to riot. His bail was set at $50,000, more than his lawyers could pay. It looked as if Abernathy might spend a long time in jail, even though he was innocent of the charge.

Confined behind bars, he found a way to continue his nonviolent protests. He went on a hunger strike. Then, after several days without food, he felt severe stomach pains. A doctor told him he was developing an ulcer, an open sore on the stomach wall. He needed to eat. Abernathy agreed to eat one egg a day until he was freed.

Inside the jail, Abernathy acted as a pastor to the other prisoners. He listened to their problems and offered advice. He also planned a family reunion for all of the Abernathys.

Meanwhile, the lawyers worked to lower his bail. The hospital workers and the local officials worked together to settle their dispute. The hospitals at last agreed to hire back the workers who had been fired. The government promised to meet with the workers' organization in cases of future grievances. The workers also received a raise in pay.

Satisfied that a victory had been won, Ralph Abernathy asked for his bail to be paid and left the Charleston jail.

The summer of 1969 was a time for family and celebration. From the scattered towns and cities where they now lived—from Cleveland, Ohio; Birmingham, Alabama; and even Los Angeles, California—Ralph Abernathy's brothers and sisters gathered with their families at the farm in Linden. They came to the reunion Ralph had planned while in jail. They played baseball, as they did when they were children. They talked about the past and planned for the future. Everyone enjoyed the reunion so much that the family came together each summer for the next 20 years.

The summer of 1969 was also a time to demonstrate for the poor. When the United States launched its first manned mission to the moon in July of that year, Ralph Abernathy led a march at the launch site, Cape Kennedy, Florida. He protested the fact that the government was spending large amounts of money to send astronauts into space, while it refused to address the problems of the poor. In a light rain, Abernathy led a group of men, women, and children, along with their dogs and mules, to the entrance of Cape Kennedy.

Seeing human beings take off for the moon was a thrill for many Americans, including Ralph Abernathy. But he reminded the nation that one-fifth of the population had too little food and clothing, poor housing, and little or no medical care. "We must improve their lot," he said.

Neil Armstrong and the other Apollo 11 astronauts brought back samples of rock from the surface of the moon. Vice President Spiro Agnew enjoyed showing those rocks to world leaders whom he met. Abernathy reflected on those events 20 years later, in an interview for the *Washington Post*. Agnew should have been "in the swamplands of Louisiana, the backwoods of Mississippi," Abernathy stated, "passing out loaves of bread to hungry children."

Chapter /Ten

The Giant-slayer

Historians are already calling the years from 1954 until 1965 "the civil rights years." During that period, the protests of the civil rights movement resulted in important legal milestones. For example, the protests prompted the Supreme Court to rule that discrimination in transportation violated the Constitution. They led to federal laws protecting the rights of all citizens to shop and dine where they wish, and to register to vote. The Southern Christian Leadership Conference was often a key force in reaching those goals.

When compared to the gains of the civil rights era, the achievements of the Southern Christian Leadership Conference after 1965 seemed small. Better working conditions for garbage collectors and hospital workers, a few new benefits for the poor—minor victories such as these improved people's lives, but they failed to capture the nation's attention. The great legal battles for racial equality had been won.

Still, some members of the Southern Christian Leadership Conference wanted their organization to do more. They decided that new management might bring fresh ideas to their cause. In 1976, they met with their president, Ralph Abernathy, and asked him to step down.

The request came as a surprise to Abernathy. It was a huge letdown to know that his staff felt unhappy with his leadership. He had always done his best for the cause of civil rights. It would be hard to walk away from an organization he founded and nurtured.

But Abernathy had learned to accept setbacks. His friends and colleagues had often heard him say, "If everything is moving smoothly in your life, you aren't doing anything." He now found a new way to serve his people—he decided to run for Congress.

Abernathy campaigned throughout the state of Georgia, asking the voters to send him to Washington. He followed a hectic schedule of speeches and public appearances. When election day arrived, though, the people of Georgia chose another candidate to be their representative.

Again, Abernathy turned a defeat into an opportunity. He repeated another of his favorite sayings: "We spend too much time trying to make a living rather than trying to make a life." For years, his work for social causes had kept him on the road. Now, his time with the Southern Christian Leadership Conference was over. His plans to enter politics had been put aside. He devoted himself to his family and church.

A fourth child, Kwame, had been born to Ralph and Juanita in 1971. Ralph Abernathy felt grateful to have time to spend with the boy. He made Kwame's breakfast each morning and drove him to school. He had seldom had time to do these things for his older children when they were growing up.

Abernathy also helped Juandalynn, Donzaleigh, and Ralph III develop their talents. Juandalynn had a fine singing voice, and he encouraged her to plan a career in opera. Donzaleigh grew up to be an actress. Her love for the plays of William Shakespeare drew her to the stage. And, said Donzaleigh in a 1993 interview, "The first time I heard Shakespeare, I heard it from my father."

After watching his father in the civil rights

movement for so many years, Ralph III dedicated himself to public service. "My speaking ability, my skills to deliver messages, and the highs and lows and the tones that I use in my voice, all of those things that individuals would normally go to school to develop, I developed naturally at home, just watching my father," said Ralph Abernathy III at his home in Atlanta in 1993. "His blood definitely runs through my veins."

Family life was rewarding, but Abernathy could not turn his back completely on social concerns. He thought about his father's belief that hard work and prosperity could solve the problems of African Americans. He conceived of a program to train black men and women in the job skills American businesses needed. Well-paying jobs, he reasoned, would help these people become productive members of society. If Abernathy's program worked, it could be a model for job training programs in other places.

The project would cost money, though. Abernathy asked several corporations and government agencies to fund the program. No one was interested.

Then Governor Ronald Reagan of California ran for president of the United States in 1980, and Abernathy felt renewed hope. Under Reagan, there had been a drop of nearly 300,000 in the number of people receiving public assistance in California. The state offered a work experience program for men and women on welfare, teaching them ways to support themselves.

Abernathy flew to Detroit, Michigan, to meet with Reagan on the campaign trail. Reagan assured the civil rights leader that he wanted very much to start a federal jobs program. He said he would work with Abernathy on the issue after he was elected. Following this meeting, Abernathy publicly endorsed Reagan's candidacy.

Reagan won the 1980 presidential election, and Abernathy waited eagerly to hear from the White House. But weeks went by, and he received no telephone calls or letters. When he tried to contact the president's staff, his calls were not returned. Reluctantly, he realized President Reagan would not help him bring prosperity to African Americans.

The economic inequality in America would weigh heavily on Abernathy's mind for the rest of his life. In July 1989, on the 20th anniversary of the first moon landing, he thought back to his protest march at Cape Kennedy. "America has refused to feed the hungry, and America has refused to wipe out poverty, and America has

Ralph Abernathy after a meeting with President Ronald Reagan in 1981

refused to provide health care," he noted sadly to David Streitfeld of the *Washington Post*. "And not only have we not found a cure for the deadly diseases of cancer and diabetes and high blood

pressure, but we have discovered new diseases."

Abernathy's own health had declined by the time he spoke those words. In 1983, while dictating a letter to his secretary, he had trouble pronouncing some words. His doctor told Abernathy he had suffered a mild stroke, and that he would recover. When the doctor examined him, however, he discovered a blockage in Abernathy's carotid artery. This large artery, located in the neck, carries blood to the brain. The blockage had to be removed, the physician told Abernathy. Left in place, it could cause a massive stroke, like the one that had killed his father so many years earlier.

Surgeons at Johns Hopkins Hospital in Baltimore, Maryland, performed the new and risky operation. The surgery was a success, but the doctors warned Abernathy that he might have more small strokes. Abernathy returned to Atlanta and resumed his duties as pastor of the West Hunter Street Church as soon as he felt well enough.

One of a minister's happiest tasks is performing weddings. On May 31, 1986, the Reverend Ralph Abernathy not only joined a couple in marriage, he gave away the bride! Donzaleigh was getting married in her father's church.

It was a day of joy, a day for welcoming new family members. For Abernathy, though, it was a day for concern. He felt fatigued, and he had trouble focusing his eyes. The next day he learned that he had experienced another small stroke.

Ralph David Abernathy was now 60 years old. His hair and mustache were growing gray. He wore steel-rimmed glasses. Glaucoma, a disorder that damages delicate structures in the eye, had affected his vision. Abernathy had reached an age at which many people decide to retire and devote their time to hobbies and relaxation. Yet he decided to take on a new challenge: writing the story of his life.

More than two decades had passed since the great campaigns of the civil rights movement. Americans growing up in the 1980s had been born after the successes of Montgomery, Birmingham, and Selma. They had never witnessed the segregation of Jim Crow laws. Many young blacks took for granted their right to shop in any store or register to vote. They seldom thought about the hard work and sacrifices of earlier generations to secure those rights.

Abernathy had been one of the people who changed American society. He had been present at rallies and marches that were now part of history. He wrote his book with young people in mind.

He described his childhood in Linden, his service in the army, and the triumphs and failures of the civil rights movement. He chronicled his friendship with Martin Luther King, Jr. Thinking about the Bible story of Joshua conquering the corrupt city of Jericho, Abernathy titled his book *And the Walls Came Tumbling Down.*

The book was published in 1989, and thousands of people welcomed the chance to read Ralph Abernathy's story. Men and women who had enjoyed his humor in his speeches were happy to find it in his book. One reviewer stated that Abernathy's "colorful details bring alive the history of the civil rights era."

Then in March 1990 the public learned that Ralph Abernathy had entered the hospital. He only expected to be there for a week. Doctors wanted to correct a chemical imbalance in his body that had been caused by a medication. His health declined rapidly, though, and the hospital stay turned into a long one. On April 17, while he was undergoing a medical test, Abernathy's blood pressure dropped. His heart stopped beating. The physicians gave him emergency treatment, but without success. Ralph David Abernathy had died.

Upon hearing the news, President George

Bush called Abernathy "a great leader in the struggle for civil rights for all Americans and a tireless campaigner for justice."

America remembered his accomplishments. Abernathy had performed "a silent labor that was very much needed," said Andrew Young from Atlanta when he heard of Abernathy's death. Abernathy was, said Young, "a jovial, profound, loving preacher who gave his life in the service of others."

Ralph Abernathy holds up a copy of his book at a press conference.

"All of us have a profound sense of loss," commented Jesse Jackson on April 22. Jackson stood outside the West Hunter Street Baptist Church, where he had just attended a memorial service for Abernathy. "We must judge him on what he meant to our struggle, and he was high up on the honor roll," Jackson added.

On April 23, 2,500 people assembled at the West Hunter Street Baptist Church, where Abernathy had been pastor for more than 30 years. Coretta Scott King and three of her children, Robert Kennedy, Jr., and many other well-known people attended the four-hour funeral service.

Sixty-four years earlier, W. L. and Louivery Abernathy had given their son the name of the biblical hero, David. Ralph Abernathy III referred to the story of David slaying the giant Goliath when he spoke about his father to the crowd. The *Washington Post* and other newspapers carried some of his words. His father had fought "the Goliath of racism," Ralph Abernathy III said. "I am the son of a giant-slayer."

Ralph David Abernathy had talked about the kind of funeral he wanted to have. He had asked that mules, the humble animals of the poor, carry his casket to the cemetery. Garlen and Clarence

Abernathy, two of his brothers, drove the green, mule-drawn wagon. The preacher's sons, Ralph and Kwame, walked ahead, holding the reins.

Abernathy had been, at heart, a simple man. He had requested that his tombstone bear a simple, two-word epitaph: "I tried."

Selected Bibliography

Books

Abernathy, Ralph David. *And the Walls Came Tumbling Down.* New York: Harper & Row, 1989.

Albert, Peter J., and Ronald Hoffman, eds. *We Shall Overcome: Martin Luther King, Jr., and the Black Freedom Struggle.* New York: Pantheon Books, 1990.

Easwaran, Eknath. *Gandhi the Man.* Petaluma, Calif.: Niligri Press, 1978.

Fager, Charles E. *Selma 1965: The March That Changed the South.* New York: Charles Scribner's Sons, 1974.

Franklin, John Hope. *From Slavery to Freedom: A History of Negro Americans.* 5th ed. New York: Alfred A. Knopf, 1980.

Hampton, Henry, and Steve Fayer. *Voices of Freedom: An Oral History of the Civil Rights Movement from the 1950s through the 1980s.* New York: Bantam Books, 1990.

Haskins, James. *The March on Washington.* New York: HarperCollins, 1993.

King, Martin Luther, Jr. *Stride Toward Freedom.* New York: Harper & Row, 1958.

Lane, Mark, and Dick Gregory. *Murder in Memphis: The FBI and the Assassination of Martin Luther King.* New York: Thunder's Mouth Press, 1993.

Lincoln, C. Eric, ed. *Martin Luther King, Jr.: A Profile*. Rev. ed. New York: Hill and Wang, 1984.

Raines, Howell. *My Soul Is Rested: Movement Days in the Deep South Remembered*. New York: G. P. Putnam's Sons, 1977.

Schulke, Flip, ed. *Martin Luther King, Jr.: A Documentary . . . Montgomery to Memphis*. New York: W. W. Norton & Company, 1976.

Sitkoff, Harvard. *The Struggle for Black Equality: 1954–1980*. New York: Hill and Wang, 1981.

Thoreau, Henry David. *Walden and "Civil Disobedience."* New York: New American Library, 1960.

Weisbrot, Robert. *Freedom Bound: A History of America's Civil Rights Movement*. New York: W. W. Norton & Company, 1990.

Wright, Roberta Hughes. *The Birth of the Montgomery Bus Boycott*. Southfield, Mich.: Charro Book Company, 1991.

Magazines

"Alabama: Double-Edged Blade." *Time*, January 16, 1956. p. 20

"And So the Poor People Came." *Life*, June 28, 1968. pp. 22–29

Good, Paul. "No Man Can Fill Dr. King's Shoes—But Abernathy Tries." *The New York Times Magazine*, May 26, 1968. pp. 28–29, 91–97

"Negroes Laughing?" *Time*, February 6, 1956. p. 21
"The South: City on Trial." *Time*, March 5, 1956.
   p. 21

Newspapers

Severo, Richard. "Ralph David Abernathy, Rights
   Pioneer, Is Dead at 64." *The New York Times*,
   April 18, 1990. p. B7
Streitfeld, David. "Footprints in the Cosmic Dust:
   Twenty Years Later, Six Voices on the Lost
   Promise of the Apollo Mission." *Washington
   Post*, July 20, 1989. p. D1

Index

Abernathy, Donzaleigh
  (daughter) 81, 89, 115,
  116, 117, 118, 152, 156
Abernathy, George (grand-
  father) 30, 33
Abernathy, James Earl
  (brother) 29
Abernathy, Juandalynn
  (daughter) 54, 78, 79, 117,
  118, 152
Abernathy, Juanita (wife)
  46, 47, 48, 50, 52, 53, 54,
  66, 78, 79, 89, 105, 112,
  117, 128, 146, 152
Abernathy, Kwame (son)
  152, 161
Abernathy, Louivery
  (mother) 26, 27, 32, 46, 47
Abernathy, Ralph David Jr.
  (son) 51
Abernathy, Ralph David III
  (son) 10, 81, 115, 116, 117,
  152, 153, 160, 161
Abernathy, Susie (sister) 29
Abernathy, W. L. (William)
  (father) 24, 25, 26, 31, 33
Agnew, Spiro 149
Alabama Freedom March
  110, 111, 113
*And the Walls Came
  Tumbling Down* 158

Aranayko, Linda 140

Bell, Ellen (grandmother) 23
Bevel, James 132
Bloody Sunday 108, 109
bombings 74, 79, 80, 83, 93,
  100, 134
Boynton, Amelia 102, 103
Brown Chapel (Selma) 102,
  103, 105, 106, 107, 109, 110
*Brown v. the Board of
  Education* 56
Brown, Edgar B. 36
Brown, H. Rap 125
bus boycott 7, 9, 15, 16, 65,
  66, 67, 68, 69, 70, 71, 72,
  74, 75, 76, 77, 78, 81, 82
Bush, George 159

Clark, Jim 102, 103
Cloud, John 107
Connor, "Bull" 83, 84, 85,
  86, 90, 92

Daley, Richard 121, 122
David, Ralph 29
Davis, Benjamin O., Sr. 37
Dexter Avenue Baptist
  Church (Montgomery)
  54, 65

Eastern Star Baptist Church
  51

Ebenezer Baptist Church (Atlanta) 50, 81
Evers, Medgar 94
"Eyes on the Prize" 12, 31, 70, 84, 100, 128

First Baptist Church (Montgomery) 52, 79, 80
Freedom Riders 82

Gandhi, Mohandas 58, 59, 60, 69, 104
garbage collectors' strike 126, 135, 150
Gaston Motel 84, 90, 93
Gayle, W. A. 73, 74
Gregory, Dick 130, 131

Hatchet, Jack 39, 41
hospital workers' strike 21, 144, 145, 146, 147, 150

Invaders 127

Jackson, Jesse 8, 119, 121, 130, 141, 142, 160
Jackson, Jimmie Lee 106, 113, 134
Jackson, Mahalia 98
Jim Crow laws 30, 31, 37, 59
Johnson, Fred 39, 41
Johnson, Lyndon 109
Jones, Juanita Odessa. See Abernathy, Juanita

Kennedy, John F. 93
Kennedy, Robert 125, 126, 142
King, A. D. 86, 93
King, Coretta Scott 54, 78, 79, 105, 128, 160
King, Martin Luther, Jr. 7, 8, 12, 13, 14, 16, 17, 18, 19, 20, 21, 50, 54, 58, 59, 60, 65, 66, 67, 68, 69, 70, 73, 74, 78, 79, 81, 84, 86, 88, 89, 92, 96, 99, 101, 102, 104, 106, 107, 108, 109, 110, 111, 112, 119, 122, 123, 125, 126, 127, 128, 129, 130, 131, 132, 133, 134, 135
Ku Klux Klan 83, 92, 93, 113

Lee, Bernard 127
Lewis, John 98, 99, 107
Lewis, Rufus 68
Liuzzo, Viola 113, 134
lunch counter sit-ins 82, 83

Malcolm X 101, 105, 134
March on Washington for Jobs and Freedom 15, 95, 96, 97, 100
Masonic Temple (Memphis) 128
Montgomery Improvement Association 7, 68, 72

Murder in Memphis 130

NAACP (National Association for the Advancement of Colored People) 61, 64

National Negro Council 36

Nix, E. D. 60, 61, 65

Parks, Rosa 7, 60, 62, 63, 64, 65, 67, 69

Patton (Captain) 39, 41

Poor People's Campaign 8, 21, 125, 126, 127, 137

poverty 21, 122, 123, 124, 125, 144, 148, 154

Project C 84, 85

Randolph, A. Philip 95, 96, 98

Ray, James Earl 132

Reagan, Ronald 153, 154

Reeb, James 109, 113

Resurrection City 140, 141, 142, 143

Robinson, Jo Ann 65

Roosevelt, Franklin 36

segregation 8, 12, 13, 15, 30, 31, 37, 55, 56, 57, 67, 74, 75, 77, 120, 124

Shelton, Robert 93

Shuttlesworth, Fred 84, 85, 92

Sixteenth Street Baptist Church (Birmingham) 100

Smith, James 126

Solidarity Day 143

Southern Christian Leadership Conference 16, 18, 20, 21, 81, 82, 84, 90, 96, 101, 102, 107, 119, 121, 122, 126, 130, 131, 132, 135, 140, 143, 146, 150, 151

Spring Street School 117

Stride Toward Freedom 7, 16, 18, 70

Student Nonviolent Coordinating Committee 98, 102, 107, 125

Supreme Court 31, 55, 56, 75, 77, 82, 124, 150

Thoreau, Henry David 58, 69

Till, Emmett 57, 58

Truman, Harry S. 55

Tuskegee Airmen 37

voting rights 16, 43, 44, 102, 104, 112, 138

Wallace, George 92, 107, 108, 110, 112

Warren, Earl 56

West Hunter Street Baptist
    Church (Atlanta) 81, 133,
    156, 160
White Citizens Council 77
Williams, Hosea 22, 107

Young, Andrew 18, 131, 159